Left-Handers' Golf Manual

Larry Nelson

Trafford rev. 12/03/2018

 www.trafford.com

North America & international
toll-free: 1 888 232 4444 (USA & Canada)
fax: 812 355 4082

This manual is dedicated to all those left-handed golfers who, despite being in a minority, can still compete with the best of them. It is for the beginner, the serious golfer and anyone who has an interest in learning how to play the game of golf.

TABLE OF CONTENTS

Acknowledgements

No book can be completed without the help of many people. I would like to thank Susan Wegner for taking the time out of her busy schedule to go through this manual with a fine tooth comb and make recommendations to improve its composition. Kent Hillesland, Hal Rolfes, Bill McAllister and Tony Frisch, also put in their two cents worth. I listened to their ideas, even if they are right handers, and a part of what is in here is a result of their ideas and recommendations. There are others who have encouraged me to go forward with this manual over the years, most of whom have been golfing partners at one time or another. I also thank them for their input.

PREFACE

After a game of golf one-day, a good friend and I were discussing how difficult it is to learn how to play golf well. He agreed it was difficult, but also said that anyone can learn to play it reasonably well if they learn the fundamentals and then stick to them when they are playing. I agreed that learning the fundamentals is the key to playing a good game of golf, but I also said that there are other obstacles one runs into in the process of learning how to play the game properly that don't make it that simple. He said, "Let me show you how easy this game is." He handed me an article, which he had picked up on the Internet. It was entitled, "Anyone Can Play Golf." If you have played golf at all, I think you'll appreciate it.

Anyone Can Play Golf.

"Once a player has mastered the grip and stance, all he has to bear in mind, in the brief two-second interval it takes to swing, is to keep his left elbow pointed in toward the left hip and his right arm stiff but not too stiff and a bit closer to the body than the left and take the club head past his left knee and then break the wrists at just the right instant while the right arm is still traveling straight back from the ball and the left arm stays glued to the body and the hips come around in a perfect circle, and meanwhile everything is mucked up unless the weight is 60 percent on the left foot and 40 percent on the right, not an ounce more or less, and at just the right point in the turn, the right knee bends in toward the left in a dragging motion until the right heel comes off the ground, but not too far, and be sure the hands are over the left foot, except that the right side of the left foot is tilted off the ground, but not too far, and be sure the hands at the top of the swing are high and the shaft points along a line parallel with the ground, and if it's a downhill lie, the shaft is supposed to be pointed downhill too, and pause at the top of the swing and count one, jerk the right arm straight down like a bell ringer yanking a belfry rope, and don't uncock the wrists too soon, and pull the right hip around in a circle, but don't let the shoulders turn with the hips, they have to be facing the hole, and now transfer the weight 60 percent to the right and 40 percent to the left, not an ounce more or less, and tilt the right foot now so the left side of it is straight, that's the one you hit against, watch out for the right hand, it's supposed to be extended, but not too stiff or the shot won't go anywhere, and don't let it get loose or you will hook, and let the wrists uncock, but don't force them, or you'll smother the shot and don't break too soon, but keep your head down, then hit the ball! That's all there is to it!"
Anonymous

Sounds like a difficult game to master doesn't it? Well, it is, but if you approach the game in a logical manner by breaking it down into its component parts, you can logically put the pieces together and overcome the major obstacles that stand in your way of making improvements in your game. The purpose of this manual is to help you do just that.

CHAPTER 1
INTRODUCTION

If you have ever tried to find manuals or books in the marketplace that provide good learning instructions for left-handed golfers, you were probably disappointed. There are some out there, but nothing compared to what is available for the right-handed golfer. As a left-handed player, I constantly hear from my right-handed golfing friends that the reason I flub some of my shots is that I am standing on the wrong side of the ball. When they buy a new club, which is advertised to hit the ball straighter and farther, they always ask, "Would you like to try it out?" The next comment is "Oh I forgot, the club head faces the wrong direction for you. My standard reply always is 1) they make golf courses hard for right-handed people (not really true, but I tell them that anyway) so they should wise up and start playing left-handed if they want to improve their game and, 2) if they want to see some real improvement in their game they should start applying the fundamentals to their entire game rather than going out and spending their hard-earned money on golf clubs that are supposed to eliminate hooks or slices or get an extra 50 yards off the tee. They tell me that if I am so smart, why don't I write a book on how to play golf? One day I said to myself that their suggestion was not a bad idea, and the result is what you have in your hands – a manual for left-handed golfers.

I have been playing golf for over 30 years. I've gone to golf schools, taken private lessons and done much on my own to improve my golf game. My handicap is currently in single digits and at this point I am content to just "hone" my game rather than spend the time it takes to lower my handicap rating any further. I don't consider myself to be an "expert" on every phase of the golf game but over the years I have acquired a good deal of knowledge on how to play the game properly. I would like to share what I have learned and hope it will help improve your game and give you some degree of satisfaction in knowing that left-handed people can play a good game of golf. If nothing else, the right-handers that you start beating consistently will be asking you for advice rather than making snide left-hander golf remarks.

So, let's begin by starting off with a little bit about origins of the game itself.

THE SPORT OF GOLF

Golf is believed to have originated in Scotland and has been played for many centuries in the British Isles. The dictionary defines golf as a game in which clubs with wooden or metal heads are used to hit a small, white (can be colored) ball into a number of holes in succession, (usually 9 or 18), situated at various distances over a course having manual or artificial obstacles, the objective being to get the ball into each hole in as few strokes as possible.

Sounds simple enough, but what is left out of the definition is the fact that playing golf is also mentally and physically demanding. It is a great sport in that it can be played by everyone in all kinds of weather be it sunshine, wind, rain, sleet and for the really hardy, a little snow. It takes your mind off your everyday cares and gives you four to five hours of exercise and relaxation. You can play golf by yourself, with your friends or with people you have never met before. You can play for fun or competitively. Usually you can find a golf course in an area near where you live, and in most locations where you travel for business or pleasure. The game never gets boring because nothing is ever the same. You are always playing your ball from a different location, and how you play the ball from that location requires thought and preparation on your part. Each shot is either a little or a lot different than your last one. When you get to the green your putts are always different because you never wind up in the same location and most greens vary enough that each putt you make requires just a little bit different speed or direction.

Those of you who have played golf know how difficult it can be to learn how to play the game properly and to make improvements. Whether you are new to the game or have been playing it for some time, most likely you have encountered more than just a little frustration in trying to make permanent, long-lasting changes that result in improvement in your driving, fairway irons, chipping, putting, and bunker play. Most of us will experience a certain level of improvement in our game during the first few years that we play golf. The majority of us will eventually reach a certain level of performance and then fluctuate around that level indefinitely.

Most of us are taught to believe that if you practice something hard and long enough, you will become better at it. You go to the driving range and hit ball after ball and then you go out and play on your favorite courses. You take numerous golf lessons. You read about the latest quick-fix cures from the pages of golf publications, or purchase the newest clubs, balls and other gadgets. You find that when all is said and done, you end up maintaining the same golf handicap for a seemingly endless period of time. You ask yourself "What the heck is it that limits my ability to lower my scores or handicap?" Or, "Why don't I get any better?" After going through all these gyrations, one might conclude that maybe there is a better way to improve our game. Guess what? There is a better way.

CONTENTS OF THE MANUAL

In this manual I will address many of the principal obstacles that stand in the way of or actually prevent you from making improvements in your game. One thing I would like to emphasize at this point is that simply taking sporadic golf lessons will not normally make significant improvements in your game. Golf courses are full of people who have had numerous golf lessons, and they are no better today than they were before the lessons began. On odd occasions, you think you see some improvement because you have a fantastic round but, as often as not, it is only a brief flickering spark of magic in your not so-good golf game. The end result is that you find yourself humbled again and back at the same level at which you started. And in some cases, you find yourself getting worse rather than better. I encourage you to take golf lessons but if you are going to invest in them, take them on an extended basis, not just the one-or two-hour lessons that most golfers take.

EQUIPMENT

Don't count on new equipment to improve your game. Granted, there have been technological advances in the equipment you use to play golf. Balls fly further, oversize drivers and irons hit the ball further and supposedly with greater accuracy. Clubs are lighter and the sweet spots are larger. You even have better tees! But the cold hard fact is the average score for 18 holes of golf, for both the amateur and the professional golfer, have barely changed over the years. According to the National Golf Foundation, the 18-hole scores for the average golfer remains where it has been for years - around 100. The average handicap index has dropped only 0.5 strokes since 2000. On the PGA tour this year, the average score of the players has risen by 0.28 strokes. For the professionals, many courses are being modified to make them more difficult but for the amateurs, you play the same courses most of the time so there is no excuse not to do better than 0.5 strokes.

IMPROVING YOUR GAME

The improvement in your golf game is determined not so much by the equipment you play with but rather by how you apply the fundamentals of the golf game to the equipment. If you learn the fundamentals of the game you can apply it to any equipment you use. How you do at nailing down the basics will determine whether you are able to make significant improvements. It is essential that you learn and practice the fundamentals outlined in this manual and that you practice them properly. This manual will address the fundamentals, in pictures and words, and give you what you need to make significant improvements in your game. Once you have the basics firmly locked into your mind and body memory, the way to make them stay there is by is by practicing. Each area of your game that takes you from tee to green will require practice. I can't emphasize the word practice too much. Improvements in your game will not come any other way.

This manual will take you through the fundamentals of establishing the proper grip, correct stance, balance, proper body pivot, ball position, aim and alignment. Following the basics, the manual will cover the proper setup routine, how to practice effectively, driving, long and short iron play, bunker play, putting, establishing a pre-shot routine, and exercises to improve your flexibility and endurance.

Please remember one thing: don't expect to read this manual and then go out and immediately lower your scores or handicap by a significant amount. It just won't happen that fast. However, if you follow this manual and practice the fundamentals outlined for each part of your game, over time you will definitely see an overall improvement in your golf game and a reduction in your handicap. The end result will be that you will get more enjoyment out of your game.

CHAPTER 2
GETTING READY TO PLAY

Every activity we participate in requires that we apply either our mental or physical capabilities, or both. If you are a beginner at any endeavor and wish to perform in a somewhat decent manner then you must learn the fundamentals that govern how best to participate fully in that activity. Once you have learned them and wish to improve further, you must then practice applying those fundamentals over and over again until they become an integral part of you. No matter what the activity, whether it is skiing, swimming, basketball, or learning a profession or skill, you must set the foundation for learning on established fundamentals if you expect to perform successfully enough to enjoy yourself.

Some people perform better in a physical activity than others. Much of this ability has to do with our basic anatomy. Tall people are more likely than short people to get into basketball at the college and professional level. A person with a 160-

pound frame is not going to be a standout Sumo wrestler or football player. All of us aren't destined to be Olympic athletes. However, one great thing about the game of golf is that your physical make-up is not really a limiting factor. You can play the game well if you are tall or short, light or heavy, male or female, young or old. I think you will agree that those physical attributes cover most of the population. It is no wonder it has become one of the most popular sports, worldwide. However, like anything else, if you want to do well at the game you must learn how to play it properly. This requires that you have a good grasp of the underlying fundamentals of the game. Once you have this, all that is required is a proper mental attitude and practice, practice and more practice.

Golf is as much a mental game as it is a physical game. It requires that you think about club selection, your set-up, where you intend to hit the ball, your approach shots to the green, your putting and a host of other things. In each case, you then have to physically execute what you have established in your mind. This is not easy to do because there is not much room for error. So how do you put it all together? To answer that question, let's start at the beginning.

LEARNING HOW TO PLAY

There are basically three ways to learn how to play golf:

- You can learn from someone who is already an accomplished golfer.
- You can read and study an instruction manual and other literature available on the subject and then go out and duplicate what you have read.
- You can learn by trial and error.

Method three is the hardest and most frustrating because you are out there flailing away with no direction and no specific objectives in mind. Believe it or not, this is the way most of us learn how to play golf. No wonder you throw your golf clubs and stomp your feet and look for the latest gimmicks to "straighten out your game".

I think all golfers have a common goal, and that is to improve the way they are currently playing. You can only attain this goal by first learning the fundamentals of the game and then applying those fundamentals on the golf course. Properly learning how to play the game of golf involves a basic learning process that must be understood and adhered to if you wish to become a better player. Building a golf game is analogous to building a house. You must first create a solid foundation. Whether a house or a golf game, they both will tumble down around you without a proper foundation. If you apply proven principles of learning toward both the mental and physical aspects of the game, there is no reason that you can't make significant improvements in your game.

SETTING GOALS FOR YOURSELF

Many golfers set unrealistic goals for themselves. It is important you recognize that if you do not have the time and energy to spend time on the practice range and practice green, you will not play golf as well as someone who does. Therefore, before getting deeply into the instruction portion of this manual, it is important that you make a personal assessment of where golf will fit into your present lifestyle. Do you want to become a competitive player? If so, you must be prepared to put in the hours of practice required achieving this goal. If you want to make some significant improvement in the way you are currently playing, then a definite amount of practice time, both on and off the golf course, must be devoted to making the necessary improvements. If you are comfortable just playing with your friends on the weekends with a few practice sessions every now and then to keep yourself one step ahead of your competitors, then your goal should be to make minor improvements and to enjoy the game at your present level of play. Be honest with yourself in this evaluation. You will find that the game of golf is much more fun when you know what you are trying to accomplish.

YOUR PRESENT GAME

The way you swing your golf clubs may not be as bad as you think it is. Your techniques may need a complete overhaul or just some minor adjustments, but keep in mind that it will take a good deal of practice to incorporate any changes that you do make into your muscle memory. There are exceptions to every rule but, generally, you will not become noticeably better overnight. As a matter of fact, there is usually a little backward movement in your game before there is forward movement. If you have been playing golf for any length of time, you will find that you are physically and mentally comfortable with what you are doing. Whether you realize it or not, there will be a tendency to initially fight the changes needed to properly learn the game and to incorporate the fundamentals. Learning to play golf correctly takes time, so be prepared to spend some of it if you want to improve your present level of play.

Recognize that a few lessons now and then with the neighborhood teaching pro, while well intentioned, may not produce the results you want. If you plan to take lessons, go for the long-term lessons where the pro has the time to teach you all the fundamentals. Once you have the basics down then use the periodic lessons for tweaking some area of your game that you want to improve. If you go into periodic lessons without having a good foundation for the basics, you may find that these lessons can present you with some temporary cures that may work for a short period of time but will eventually fail or, even worse, create additional problems.

If you are willing to work to reach a higher level in your golf game, then applying the fundamentals presented in this manual will help you reach that level. The only variable in getting where you want to be is you.

BE READY TO MAKE SOME CHANGES

Each of us learns to perform various tasks at a different rate. We also have different ways of learning. In addition to how you learn, you will find that golf also may have a different priority for you than it does for your relatives, friends and acquaintances. The result is that there are no set time frames for improvement. You can take as long as you want (within reason) to make the changes needed for improvement. One thing is certain: if you are willing to accept instruction and make a dedicated effort to practice what is required to improve, there is no question that you will get better. As your grip, posture, stance and overall knowledge of how to play various shots improve, so will your confidence in your game. There will be more smiles, and less frowns.

For many of us, if we make a swing change and don't notice immediate improvement in the way we strike the ball, we quickly abandon the swing change and go back to our old ways of doing things. How many times on a golf course have you changed your grip, your backswing, your stance, ball position, alignment, etc., to see if the changes will improve your game? I'm sure the answer to that question is, "many times". What normally happens is that either you go back to your old way of doing things or you adopt the change you have made. Sometimes those changes are for the better because, whether you recognized it or not, you may have hit upon the proper correction and just don't know it. It takes time before any changes you make can be incorporated physically and mentally into your golf game. One word of caution at this point - it may not be productive to experiment with changes during a golf game. If you make more than one or two, you'll never know which one helped and which one really fouled up your game. If you want to try the change, go to the practice range with one objective in mind, and that is to work on that change to see if it will improve that area of your game.

DON'T EXPECT TOO MUCH

The golf swing is a physical motion that involves almost every part of your body. Developing a proper swing requires good co-ordination between all parts. Since a golf swing is not a normal part of our everyday body motions, it will take practice on your part to get the body and mind to function harmoniously so you make the swing automatically and do it correctly each time. If you have ever participated in other sports like baseball, skiing or tennis, you know that there is a significant learning curve involved in becoming proficient at them. However, you eventually get to a point where you don't have to think about every motion involved. It becomes automatic. Just imagine what it would be like if you were playing baseball and had to stop and think about how you were going to catch the fly ball coming to you in left field or if you were playing tennis how you had to pause and think about how to hit a tennis ball back to your opponent. There is no time to think. It is a reflexive action that comes about because of the training and practice that went into making those physical reactions a part of your mental process. So it is with golf.

This manual will provide you with the basics necessary to play golf properly. What you must do is take what is presented in this manual and transfer the information into a motor skill. There are no shortcuts to learning how to swing a golf club properly, how to chip, get out of a bunker or putt. All of these fundamentals must be learned from the bottom up. This will take proper practice, repetition and time. Also be prepared that these changes will likely feel uncomfortable for a lengthy period of time before you adjust fully to the change. I think you will agree that once you have the fundamentals down, honing those skills is not just a one or two day exercise. It is a long term commitment.

CHAPTER 3
GOLF ETIQUETTE

No book on golf would be complete without discussing the principles of golf etiquette. Etiquette fundamentally prescribes and restricts the ways in which people interact with each other and show their respect for one another by conforming to the norms of society. In other words, consideration should be shown for one another on the golf course.

Golf, since its inception, has been considered a gentleman's game, and has an established code of conduct. Those of you who are seasoned golfers know most of the more important rules of etiquette, but to refresh your memory and to educate the beginners, the following is a short guide on the rules for proper behavior.

1. Take care of the golf course because it receives a lot of wear and tear. Repair your fairway divots (Fig 3-1 and Fig 3-2) either with the divot that flew 10 yards down the fairway or with the seed and sand mixture that some courses provide with their golf carts. When replacing a divot, don't just lay it in there with your hand. Make sure that you tamp it down firmly with your foot so that the grass has an even chance to gain a foothold to grow back.

Fig 3-1

Fig 3-2

2. When someone is playing a shot, don't stand where you can be seen in their peripheral vision. Stand behind them and slightly to the right or left so they can't see you. If you are talking to someone, stop while the person is addressing the ball and completing his or her swing. Golf requires a good deal of concentration, and distraction from other players is not something that helps one focus on hitting the golf ball properly.

3. For safety purposes, don't stand to close to or ahead of someone when they are making their shot. It is not only disconcerting to the golfer, but an errant golf ball could hit you. There is also a chance a golf club could fly out of a person's hand if the grip is wet or not gripped tightly enough.

4. Rake the sand traps (Fig 3-3) after you have hit your ball. There is nothing more frustrating to the golfers behind you than to find their ball is lying in your footprint. Leave the bunker in the same condition that you would like to find it. Leave the rakes on the edge of the sand trap, lying parallel to the edge.

Fig 3-3

5. Repair your ball marks on the green and around the fringe of the green. (Fig 3-4 and Fig 3-5). Use a tee or one of the tools that is specifically designed for the job. A damaged area from a ball mark, if not repaired promptly, takes about three weeks to get back to its original condition. If done properly, it will repair itself overnight. Look for a few areas that other golfers neglected to repair and fix those also. It only takes a second of your time.

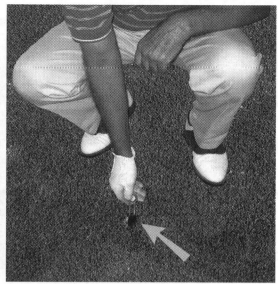

| Fig 3-4 | Fig 3-5 |

6. Repair your ball marks correctly. See Fig 3-6 and Fig 3-7.

CORRECT
Pull all sides of the ball mark into the center. This should close the hole. Then gently tap the ball mark down with the head of the putter.

INCORRECT!
Pulling up on the center or the sides will leave the center raised. The mover can then clip off the top. This can cause damage to the roots

| Fig 3-6 | Fig 3-7 |

7. Don't drag your feet on the greens. Spike marks, whether from soft spikes or metal spikes, can do some significant damage. If you do drag your feet, fix the damaged area. Tamp down any spike marks that may be around the hole.

8. Don't walk in another player's putting line. Fig 3-8. Impressions from your shoes can make a difference on the accuracy of their putt. Either step over the player's putting line or walk behind the player who will be putting.

9. Mark and remove your ball from the green if it is in or around the line of another player's putting direction.

10. When you remove the flag from the cup on the green, lay it down. Tossing a flag can dig into the green, leaving a mark that is just the same as a ball mark.

Fig 3-8

11. If you are riding in a cart, follow the rules prescribed by the golf course. These rules change, depending on the condition of the course. If the course is wet, you may have a 90-degree cart rule or be requested to keep the carts on the path that day. The next day the course may permit carts to be fully on the fairways. Always keep your carts away from the greens.

12. Slow play is one of the more frustrating situations to a golfer. There are some simple rules you can follow to make sure you are not being cursed by the group behind you.

●If your ball goes into the rough (Fig 3-9)

Fig 3-9

don't spend excessive time looking for it. Take a couple of minutes to look for it and then move on. If your partners are on the opposite side of the course, they should not spend the time to help to find your ball. Only those in your same general vicinity should help you look.

20

●After hitting your ball, walk directly to it so you are ready to hit immediately when it is your turn. It's not necessary to walk to your partner's ball to keep them company and then cross to the other side of the fairway to hit yours.

●If the players behind you are pressing you and there is an opening ahead, offer to let them play through. They may decide not to, but the gesture is what is important.

●If you are walking, when you reach the green leave your clubs on the same side as the next tee. The same goes for your cart if you are riding. This may seem like a trivial item, but there are many large greens out there and you can speed things up if you don't have to walk all the way around one when you are done putting.

13. If you see an area on the golf course that needs some attention, take the time to report it to the proper person at the clubhouse when you finish your round. They may already know of the problem but it doesn't hurt to report it anyway. They will appreciate your concern for the golf course.

14. Hitting into golfers ahead of you (Fig 3-10) is not only inconsiderate but also dangerous. Wait until you are sure they are far enough away from you so there is

Fig 3-10

no chance your ball will come close to them. Getting hit by a golf ball is not fun as some of you well know. It is very annoying to have golf ball roll by you on the fairway or bounce off your bag or cart. It's also not appropriate to have your golf ball land on the green while the group ahead of you is putting. Wait until the golfers ahead of you are off and away from the green before hitting your approach shot.

RULES OF GOLF
I will not cover the rules of golf in this manual because they are too extensive to do so. You can find the PGA rules of golf at your local golf course or golf equipment store. They are also available over the Internet at various web sites.
Observing the few simple rules of etiquette discussed above, using your common sense and being considerate of other golfers on the course will make the day enjoyable for everyone. The game is difficult enough as it is, and any inconsiderate acts on your part will only lower their enjoyment level.

CHAPTER 4
THE FUNDAMENTALS

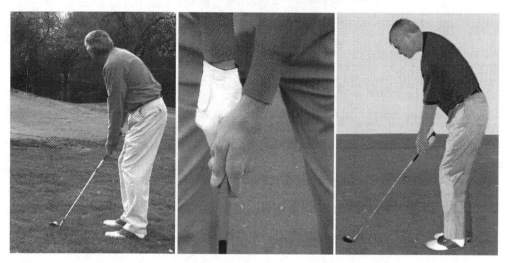

Ever notice what the professional golfers are doing before, after and sometimes during rounds of golf? They are working on some fundamental of their golf game that they feel needs improvement. If it is your intent to improve your game, then take a hint from the professionals – direct your efforts toward working on the fundamentals of the game. How you hold the club, where you aim the clubface and the way you stand will determine the direction and flight of the golf ball. It will also determine how solidly the club comes into contact with the ball. A fundamentally sound setup won't guarantee a perfect swing, but weak fundamentals will guarantee that you'll never improve. Only when you get the finer points of the key areas down– grip, posture, alignment and ball position - to where you no longer have to think about them on every shot should you turn your attention to how you swing the golf club.

Let's look at the four things I just mentioned that are an integral part of every golf shot that you make – grip, posture, alignment and ball position.

GRIP - It is not important that you have a "perfect grip" to play golf successfully, but to become a good player you must understand the function and the importance of the grip. The grip is your body's physical connection to the golf club. It controls the clubface and, therefore, dictates the position of the clubface at the moment of impact. Your hands are the only contact that you will make with the golf club, so that contact must be made correctly or you will introduce unwanted errors into your game. Don't grip the club too tightly. The grip should be just tight enough that the club does not slip in your hands with a full swing of the club. This will permit you to maintain the flexibility required in the hands and wrists to bring the club head through the ball properly. This flexibility will also result in a more powerful swing, because the wrist action on the downswing will result in higher club head speed.

POSTURE – Power and control in golf come from a balanced setup. In general, make sure your weight is evenly distributed front to back and left to right.

AIM AND ALIGMENT – Ensure that your shoulders, hips and feet are in line with the intended flight of the ball. Be precise in your alignment. Even if your swing is done well, if the ball travels in an errant direction the good swing isn't of much value.

BALL POSITION – The width of your stance, and the position of the ball in relation to your hands and feet, will vary as you change from shorter to longer clubs.

HOW TO ESTABLISH THE PROPER GRIP

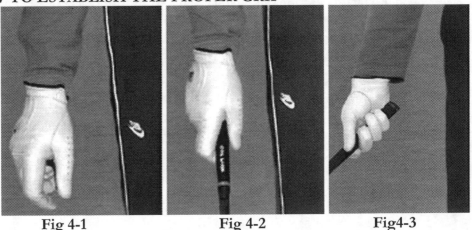

| Fig 4-1 | Fig 4-2 | Fig4-3 |

To grip the club properly, use the following procedure:

24

•Let your right hand hang down to your side so that it assumes its natural position. (Fig 4-1).

•Place the hand over the grip in this natural position (Fig 4-2). This position will allow you to support the club during your swing and square the clubface at impact.

•When you grip the club as shown in Fig 4-2, the hand should be on the club so that the shaft runs from the pad on your palm and diagonally through the lower joint of your index finger. Close your hand around the grip. Apply pressure to the grip with the last three fingers of the right hand so that the club is pressed firmly into the hand. As you look down at your hand, the thumb should be slightly favoring the left side. (Fig 4-3).

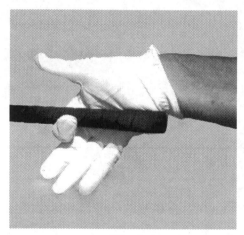
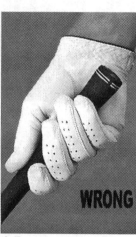

Fig 4-4   **Fig 4-5**

•To get a good feel for this right hand grip, pick up the club, hold it horizontally, and then balance it between the heel pad in your hand and the index finger as shown in (Fig 4-4.)

•This is the correct position in the hand. To help you remember this position, open your hand and with a martex pen run a line across your glove from the heel pad through the lower portion of the index finger. You can use this line to consistently place the grip in the correct position in your hand. The correct and incorrect positions for the right hand grip are shown in Fig 4-5.

•Next, move your left hand forward from its natural hanging position and place it on the club below your right hand. The club should be held the same way — between the pad of the hand and the index finger.

●With the palm of the left hand, press the thumb of the right hand firmly against the grip. Make sure the pressure on the grip with the right hand is primarily with the last three fingers. Fig 4-6 shows the proper position for the hands when gripping the club. The image on the right shows an open hand so you can see the position of the right hand thumb on the club shaft. .

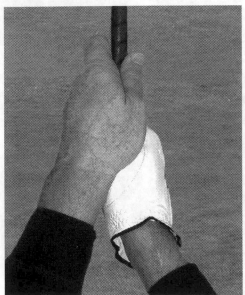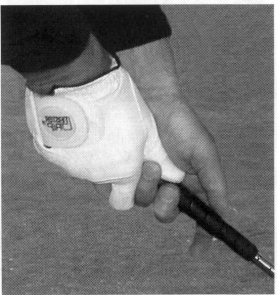

Fig 4-6

GRIP TYPES

There are three grip types and grip positions commonly used for tying the hands together on the golf club. The most popular grip type is the Vardon, or overlapping grip (Fig 4-7) wherein the small finger rests on the notch between the right index and middle fingers. Alternatively, the finger can be entwined with the right index finger for an interlocking grip (Fig 4-8) or held like a baseball bat (Fig 4-9) with a 10-finger grip. The 10-finger grip is considered a power grip, as it promotes more forearm rotation through impact with the ball. Regardless of which grip you choose, the fundamentals of how to hold the club in your hands applies to all three grips.

Overlapping grip	Interlocking grip	Baseball grip
Fig 4-7	Fig 4-8	Fig 4-9

GRIP POSITIONS

There are three variations to each of the grips described above – the weak grip, the neutral grip and the strong grip. I recommend that you don't use the weak and strong grips because they make it very difficult to return the clubface to a square position at impact.

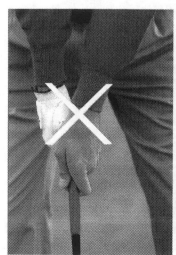
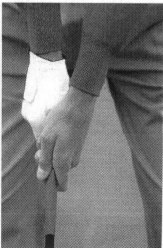
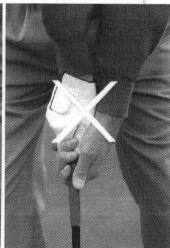

Weak Grip	Neutral Grip	Strong Grip
Fig 4-10	Fig 4-11	Fig 4-12

Weak Grip Fig 4-10 – Your grip is weak if your hands are turned too far around to the right.

Neutral grip Fig 4-11 – Ideally both hands should be in a neutral position. Fig 4-6 also shows a neutral grip.

Strong grip Fig 4-12 – Your grip is strong if your hands are turned too far to the left. A slight strong left hand is acceptable, but from the front you should never be able to see more than three knuckles. If your shots are going off line, look at your hand position because the grip influences the impact position of the clubface with the ball.

1. A simple way to check for a neutral grip at home is to do the following:

Stand in front of a mirror and place each hand on the grip. Place the right hand on the grip first. The "V" formed by the index finger and the thumb should point upward to a point somewhere between your left eye and left shoulder.

2. Place the left hand on the grip. The "V" should point to the same area between your left eye and left shoulder. If they are not in this position they are not properly aligned. Rotate each hand until each of them is in the proper position. As stated previously, don't grip the club too tightly. Imagine holding a banana in your hands and squeezing it just hard enough not to crush it. You want a firm grip with the correct fingers but not with the entire hand. Your arms should remain relaxed to permit your wrists to cock freely.

ADDRESSING THE BALL WITH NORMAL POSTURE

Correct posture, along with knowing how to address the ball properly, is critical to playing solid golf. The body angles that you create when you address the ball determine what you can and can't do with your swing. Done correctly, your posture sets your body at the proper height and distance from the ball. Setting your stance so that you are properly aligned will determine the direction your golf ball takes off the clubface. It is imperative in your golf swing that you maintain the same height from the point of addressing the ball, through your backswing, and then downward through impact with the ball. Two popular methods for establishing the proper posture and addressing the ball are outlined below.

In discussing how to address the ball, I will be repeating much of the discussion on posture, since the two are closely associated with each other. The position of the body with respect to the ball is extremely important. Standing too close to the ball so that your elbows are at your sides promotes picking up the club too soon. This can cause a reduction in the coil in your backswing and produce an outside-to-inside swing. The result is a slice. If you stand too far from the ball and have to "reach" for it you will lose power in your swing and most likely will not hit the ball squarely in the center of the clubface.

POSTURE

| Fig 4-13 | Fig 4-14 |

- With your arms hanging naturally at your side, step into the ball with the left foot. Place the club on the ground behind the ball with the right hand. Make sure the face of the club is perpendicular to the line of intended flight.
- Bend slightly at the waist and place the left hand on the club to form the grip that you intend to use. ***Bend over at the hips, not the waist.*** The angle on your spine, Fig 4-14 and Fig 4-15 will vary, depending on your flexibility, but should be approximately 20 to 25 degrees. The bend will force your rear end outward. This angle should stay constant from address, through the backswing, through the downswing and into the follow-through.
- Step into place with the right foot so that both feet are close together.

6 to 9 degrees from vertical

| Fig 4-15 | Fig 4-16 |

- With your legs straight and locked at the knees, spread your feet apart so they are the width of your shoulders.
- Bend your knees and raise the sole of the club so that it is just slightly off the ground or just barely touching. The amount of bend in the knees will change as the length of the golf club changes. The spine angle, however, will remain the same. Your head, in all cases, will be behind the ball. This will put your right shoulder slightly higher than the left and also give you a small amount of tilt in your spine to the left. The width of your stance will change with different club lengths (See Ball Position on page 35).
- As shown in Fig 4-16, your body should tilt slightly to the left. To get an idea of the proper sideways tilt, stand up straight and look straight down at your belt buckle. Then, without shifting the weight on your feet, tilt to the left until your eyes and your belt buckle are pointing to your right instep. That is how much side bending you should feel when you address the ball. The side tilt away from the target line moves your center of gravity behind the ball and promotes the proper weight shift onto your back foot on the backswing.

●On the downswing, the weight will transfer from the back to the front foot. During this whole process, the only thing that will vary is the ball position. Suffice it to say that in your stance the ball will be closer to your front foot with the woods, more toward center for the long to mid-range irons, and slightly toward the left heel for the short irons.

One of the common faults golfers have is the tendency to stand too upright when they address the ball and, therefore, their spine is too centered. This can cause a weight shift, which goes to the front foot on the backswing and to the back foot on the downswing. The result will be that the club bottoms out too early and the shot is too fat or thin. The body should rotate around your waist and hips. Keep your knees and hips at the same level throughout your swing.

AIM AND BODY ALIGNMENT

Most golf shots are missed before the golf club even moves away from the ball. Your swing can be picture perfect, but if you are not properly aligned the ball will not go where you intended. It will wind up somewhere you least expect it to and often this is in the rough, in a lateral hazard or out of bounds. How you align yourself for the golf shot is one of the most important elements of any golf swing. Amazingly enough, it is often one of the last things people consider when correcting direction problems in their game.

Proper alignment is a critical part of a successful golf swing. Time and attention paid to this area of your game can make a significant difference in the quality of your golf game. With a proper setup the likelihood that you will hit a reasonable shot is fairly good, even if your swing is not picture perfect. If you set up incorrectly, you will hit a bad shot even if your swing is perfect. To achieve correct alignment, it is mandatory that you align your feet, knees, hips, shoulders, forearms and eyes in a parallel line. Try to visualize the proper alignment position at address, and align the leading edge of the clubface perpendicular to the ball's target line.

The square ness of the body to the intended flight path of the ball has a major bearing on the swing path. If your body is aligned to the left, you will tend to swing the golf club to the left. If it is aligned to the right, you will swing the club to the right. **In the alignment process the most important part of your body is the shoulders.** Many of you probably spend most of the alignment process looking at your feet. The alignment of the feet is important, but it is the shoulders that determine how you will swing the club because the arms and hands are attached to the shoulders. It is the arms that swing the club and since they are attached to the shoulders, the arms will go in the direction of the shoulders. Therefore, when you are establishing your alignment, concentrate on the shoulders first and then the hips, knees, hands and feet. Your shoulders should be square and parallel to the target line. Since you can't see your shoulders to determine if they are properly aligned, one thing you can do is place the shaft of the club across your upper chest. To line up your shoulders, align the shaft so it points in the direction you intend to hit the ball. You can also do the same for the hips to make sure they are aligned with the shoulders.

AIMING THE CLUBHEAD FIRST

An excellent way to establish proper alignment is to use the club head as the first step in the alignment process. Many experienced golfers feel that when you take your grip and stance first, and then lower the club head to the ball, it is more difficult to precisely align your club head. When using the clubface for your initial alignment with your irons use the following guidelines:

| **Fig 4-17** | **Fig 4-18** | **Fig4-19** |

- With your arms extended (Fig 4-17), stand to the side of the ball and focus on your target line.
- Lower the club with the right hand and set the bottom edge of the clubface behind the ball so that the heel and toe are flat on the ground. Make sure the heel, midpoint and toe are perpendicular to your target line. This will make sure the clubface points directly at your target.

32

- Once you have correctly set the clubface (Fig 4-18), step into position with the left foot. This will keep your body open to the target so that you can focus on it. Place your left hand on the grip, making sure not to alter the clubface position.
- Move the right foot into position (Fig 4-19) and set your feet at the proper shoulder width with your weight equally distributed between both feet. Balance on the balls of your feet, not on the heels or toes.
- Fine-tune your stance to make sure the clubface is centered on the ball and that your arms are relaxed and your grip on the club is not too tight. Set your shoulders, hips, knees, feet, forearms and eyes in a line parallel to the target line. When you feel you are properly aligned, take one last look down the target line to satisfy yourself that all parts of your body are in alignment.

DISTANCE FROM THE BALL

The following exercise is a good one to use to ensure you are standing the proper distance from the ball. You can also use it for a full address of the ball.

FRONT
Fig 4-20

SIDE
Fig 4-21

- Preset a full arm extension at address by holding the club as shown in Fig 4-20.
- Keep the arms soft and relaxed.
- The left shoulder should be a little lower than the right; elbows in front of the chest.

- With your arms extended, stand to the side of the ball. (Fig 4-21) and focus on your target line.
- Step into your address with your feet together.
- Bend at the hips and lower the club head behind the ball.
- Your arms and hands should be hanging directly below your shoulders.
- Spread your feet to shoulder width and then bend your knees.
- The stance for this shot is slightly open. The ball is located toward the back foot.
- Position the ball in the proper location for the desired shot; i.e., forward, centered or back in your stance.
- Take a last look down the target line making sure your shoulders, hips, arms and hands are pointing in the proper direction. Fig 4-22 and Fig 4-23 show the proper position for an iron shot to the green.

Fig 4-22

Fig 4-23

BALL POSITION

The term ball position refers to where the ball sits on the ground with respect to your stance. The key body parts in ball position are the right and the left foot. Fig 4-24 shows the relative position of the ball with respect to the feet, depending upon which club you are using.

Follow the guidelines below for establishing the correct ball position for the various clubs:

Driver   Five Iron   Pitching Wedge

Fig 4-24

●Your widest stance will come when you are hitting a driver, but you should always make sure it is not wider from heel to heel than your shoulders. For the driver, place the ball one or two inches back from the heel of your right foot.

●For the mid-irons, narrow your stance and move the ball toward the center of your stance.

●The shorter swing produced by shorter clubs requires a narrower stance. The ball is positioned left of centerline toward the left heel.

Once you have reached the point where you have a good grasp of all four fundamentals i.e. grip, posture, alignment and ball position, you are well on your way to making satisfying improvements in your golf game.

CHAPTER 5
THE GOLF SWING

There are many differing opinions as to what constitutes a proper golf swing. One thing that everyone does agree on is that it involves almost every part of your body. The correct swing occurs when all of the right body parts are moving in the correct manner at the right time. When you swing, your body rotates and your arms and legs are in motion, and how all of them move and rotate affects the outcome of your swing. When swinging a golf club, there are two things that are crucial - the amount of lower body motion you use in the backswing (very little) and the amount of lower body motion you use in the downswing (a great deal). If you can get all the right body parts moving in the proper direction at the right time, you should be able to move the club head into the ball in a consistent manner.

Chapter 4 covered the fundamentals of the grip, posture, alignment, ball position and balance points. In this Chapter you will incorporate all of these fundamentals into executing a golf swing. The swing process is outlined in simple steps that will help you to set up properly and give you the best chance of achieving a proper swing. One helpful tip that will help you is that when going through the instructions outlined in this and the following chapters, have a golfing friend go to the practice range with you. They can read each of the itemized steps, observe what you are doing and correct you when you are not following the directions. You can then switch positions and do the same for them. Doing this will help you see the errors being made and the corrections needed. Also, practicing these steps in front of a full-length mirror in the privacy of your own home is a good way to get the fundamental swing motions down.

KEY SWING POSITIONS
When hitting a golf ball, the golf swing must travel through specific and definable swing positions. These positions, which are fundamental to executing the right golf swing, are the key to the execution of a proper swing, and all of them take place in a matter of two to three seconds. The successful swing occurs when you are able to move through all the fundamental swing positions in a smooth and systematic manner. This is not an easy task to accomplish. However, the cold hard fact is that unless you make the proper moves in each position, the final outcome of your swing will be less than optimal. One good move on your swing, such as the proper take away and upper body rotation, normally leads to another. The opposite is also

true - one bad move leads to another. Once you know the proper moves to make at each position, and you are able to execute these moves, you will see a significant improvement in your golf swing. How do you achieve a proper swing? Following the instructions outlined will get you started in the right direction.

Remember to practice these fundamentals so they become second nature to you.

GENERAL RULES FOR PROPER SETUP AND ALIGNMENT

- For a shorter iron, the heels of your feet should be as wide apart as your hips. Your stance will get wider as the club shaft gets longer. Be certain that your arms are relaxed and hanging directly below your shoulders - do not reach with your arms or allow them to crowd your body. Hold the grip just tight enough that the club will not come out of your hands when you swing. Tension will destroy the golf swing. You can't be tense and expect to swing to a good finish position. Remember to relax your arms and hands.
- For a driver and woods, your right toe is rotated forward approximately 30 45 degrees. The left foot is slightly flared around 20 degrees.
- Your weight should be balanced equally between your left and right foot.

- The weight is distributed on the balls of your feet.
- The proper knee flex should give you the sensation of resting your rear end on a barstool.
- Your head is behind the ball.
- Your left shoulder is slightly lower than your right shoulder.

Practice these points and learn to master them before you get to the golf course. Do this by practicing in front of a mirror or at the driving range. Your goal should be to make this setup as automatic as possible. The only way to do this is to practice it repeatedly.

1. THE TAKE AWAY

FRONT

SIDE

- Draw the club shaft back low to the ground.
- Keep left knee flexed.
- Move the shoulders, arms, hands and golf club in a one-piece take away.
- The hands should move outside the left foot.
- Weight begins to shift to the inside of the left foot.
- The left knee is still flexed.

- Keep your spine angle the same as at your address.
- The club shaft is approximately parallel to the ground.
- Club head is in line with the hands and aimed slightly left of the target line.

2. LEFT ARM PARALLEL TO THE GROUND

FRONT

SIDE

- Your head has shifted to the left.
- The wrists are cocked.
- The club shaft is 90 degrees to right arm.
- The right heel is on the ground.
- Weight is on the inside of the left foot.
- Your wrists are cocked.

- The left knee is flexed.
- Spine angle is the same as at set-up.
- Your right wrist is flat.
- The left wrist is bent.

3. TOP OF THE BACKSWING

FRONT

SIDE

- Your shoulders have rotated 90 degrees.
- Hips rotate to approximately a 45-degree angle.
- Your right arm is on the same plane as your shoulders.
- Tension is on the inside of the left thigh.
- Your head is level (same as setup).

- Your spine angle is same as at address.
- Shoulders are rotated 90 degrees to the spine.
- Weight is on the inside of the left foot.
- Your left elbow is pointed at the left hip.

4. DOWNSWING

FRONT

SIDE

- Weight has shifted slightly to the right side.
- Hips are finished moving laterally and are now beginning to rotate.
- Your left elbow is in line with left hip.
- The club shaft is parallel to the ground.
- Your right and left knees are flexed

- Your spine angle is the same as at address.
- The left knee is flexed.
- Your hands are close to the left thigh.
- The club head is in line with or slightly behind the hands.
- The toe of the golf club is pointing up.

CLUBHEAD AT IMPACT

FRONT

- The left elbow, left hip, and left knee are in line with each other.
- Keep your head behind the ball.
- Your weight is approximately 70 percent on the front foot.
- Keep your right wrist flat.
- Your hips should be about 20-40 degrees open and your shoulders 0-10 degrees open.
- Left heel is raised from the ground.

6. THE FOLLOW THROUGH

SIDE

- Don't keep your head fixed through impact. When your shoulders turn through the ball, let them move your head around and up naturally.
- Your weight should be outside the right foot near the heel.
- Your right knee is straight and the left knee is flexed.
- Your thighs are together.
- Rotate so that you come up onto the left toe.
- Your left hip will be more toward target than the right.
- Your eyes should be looking over your left arm.
- Your left arm is on the same plane as the shoulders.
- Make sure your hands and arms are relaxed, your elbows folded and that your hands wind up outside the right shoulder.

The finishing position occurs after the ball has left the clubface. Because of this, many players feel that the follow-through is not that important. ***Don't make this mistake.*** The finishing position is the culmination of the proper swing sequence. If you cut it short and don't follow through, you will find that you begin to slow your swing down even before you hit the ball. This can throw your body out of position, the result being poor contact and a bad shot. The follow-through is not an automatic part of the swing. It requires practice, as do all the other key positions of a proper golf swing. Make sure you swing through the ball. You will see an improvement in your rhythm, timing and tempo, and better ball direction and ball flight when you achieve a good finishing position. Practice in front of a mirror to ensure you are in the correct positions on your swing.

Making a full backswing so that you reach a horizontal position at the top is difficult for many people because they lack either the body or wrist flexibility. If you want to make a fuller backswing make sure you are using a neutral grip so that your wrists can cock freely, and then loosen your right hand grip. This lighter grip will allow the weight of the club head to pull the shaft into a more horizontal position. Near the top of the swing, the lower portion of the grip will move more into the fingers of your right hand.

A common mistake made during the golf swing is rising up during the backswing and then compensating for this by bending the knees a little more on the downswing. In other words, you become taller and then shorter during the swing process. See Figs. 5-1 and 5-2. If the up and down motion is not equal you either

Fig 5-1   Fig 5-2

wind up hitting the ball thin or fat. If you do both, you might get lucky and have each error cancel out the other. The result is that you hit the ball correctly even though you don't realize what you have done. Remember, the golf ball is only 1.67 inches, or 4.25 centimeters, in diameter, so straightening or bending a little during the golf bending can cause untold misery in your golf game. Proper posture is critical to a successful golf swing.

The six steps outlined above describe the mechanics of a proper golf swing. However, along with the golf swing mechanics you also have to consider three other factors that influence the golf swing: namely, tempo, rhythm and timing.

TEMPO

Your golf swing should have two slow points and one fast point. The first slow point is the take away, after which the club builds up speed to the top of the backswing. The second slow point is the start of the downswing, which should match the speed of the take away. Many golfers get into trouble at this point because they tend to start down much faster than they bring the club back. This is a good way to get your body out of rhythm. Picture this. Instead of a golf club in your hands, you have a broom with its handle cut off so that it is the same length as your club. You are going to swing that broom like a golf club to sweep a sidewalk. This would require that you have a nice smooth swing for two reasons. First, the broom has enough surface area so that wind resistance will slow down your forward motion and, second, in order to sweep the broom along the sidewalk you have to follow through with your swing. Swing your golf club with the same tempo.

RHYTHM

The key to achieving good rhythm is coordinating the speed of the body turn with the speed of the arms, both back and through. Most golfers start their hands too quickly, swinging them to the top before the body completes its backswing turn, then jerking them out ahead on the downswing. This leads to weak, inconsistent ball striking, as the power and control of the big muscles are left behind. Focus on letting the speed of your body rotation set the pace of the swing rather than the arms and hands. To synchronize your arms and your body, practice making continuous swings, back and through, starting with short, pendulum-type motions and gradually increasing the length with each repetition.

After just a few swings, you'll notice how the hands move in a smooth rhythm with the body. As the motion continues, centrifugal force synchronizes the pull on the hands and body. Strive for this coordinated feeling when you go back to your normal swing.

TIMING

Your backswing and your forward swing should take the same amount of time. Since the forward swing is twice as long as the backswing, acceleration of the club head is required to reach the end of your follow through. Maximum acceleration should be at the point of contact with the ball. One way to practice your timing is to use a normal speed count of 1 –2 – 3 to shoulder level on the backswing, and then the same 1 – 2 – 3 to the opposite shoulder level on the downswing. Since the forward swing must cover twice the distance as the backswing you will have to increase the velocity of the club head as is comes through the ball in order to complete the swing on the count of three. This will improve your timing and also improve your rhythm at the same time. After using the counting method in your swing for a period of time you will find that your timing (and tempo) will be firmly implanted in your mind.

CHAPTER 6
THE DRIVER AND FAIRWAY WOODS

It is essential that you consistently hit the ball onto the fairway off the tee if you want to reduce your score and lower your handicap. Good drives set the tone for your overall golf game. You know the feeling when you slice one into the rough, land in a sand trap or roll the ball 30 yards down the fairway. This feeling, whether you recognize it or not, can carry over into the next shot. From a psychological standpoint you have that little bit of doubt in your mind that your next shot might not go so well either.

If you are playing competitively or just trying to beat your buddies, a poor drive puts you on the defensive. Most of the bad drives you make are a result of improper setup. For the driver, the setup is different than for every other club in your bag.

The swing plane for the driver, when you swing it properly, has a much flatter plane than your other clubs. At address, it is important that you extend your arms away from your body so that you have the feeling of "reaching" for the ball. This reaching will promote a flatter and more rounded swing plane, which results in a shallow approach to impact with the ball. A good rule to follow when your stance is complete is to make sure your hands are directly below your eyes when you look down as shown in Fig 6-1.

A common mistake players make is to keep the arms tight against the body. This is correct for the irons, but not the driver. Arms tight against the body will result in an upright swing plane and a steep angle of attack, causing the club head to hit the ground rather than sweep through the impact area. So, let's look at posture, stance, form, and position needed to complete a successful drive from the tee.

Weight distribution should be 60% on the front foot and 40% on the back foot. Most likely this is contrary to what you have learned but balance studies show that a better weight shift is achieved when the setup is on the right side and the body turns away from the ball on the backswing.

So lets look at posture, stance, form, and position needed to complete a successful drive from the tee.

POSTURE AND CLUB POSITION

Driver	Iron
Fig 6-1	Fig 6-2

Fig 6-1 and Fig 6-2 show the relative positions for the driver and an iron. Notice the position of the hands for the driver versus the iron. With the driver you move your hands and arms away from the body so that you have the feeling that you are reaching for the ball. This will promote a more rounded swing plane, which will result in a shallow sweeping approach to the ball. Keeping the arms tight against the body will produce an upright swing plane and a steep angle of approach to the ball.

GENERAL GUIDELINES FOR USING THE DRIVER

To assure that you set up your driver properly every time, it is important that you follow a set routine. Follow the guidelines below:

30-45 Degrees

- Place your feet together ball rests in the middle of your stance.

- Move your right foot forward an inch or two and flare it out approximately 30 to 45 degrees. Flare left foot.

- Move the left foot back so your stance is the width of your shoulders. Weight is 40% on the back foot 60% on the right foot. Stance is partially closed. Slight body tilt to the left.

ONCE IN POSITION, DO THE FOLLOWING:

- Check for a snug right-hand grip.
- Align the body a little to the left of target.
- Relax – inhale to relieve any tension you may have.
- Waggle the club to relieve any tension in your arms and hands.
- Extend a firm right arm. Turn the hips as you move the club back from the ball.
- Swing with tempo and rhythm

50

STANCE AND BALL POSITION FOR DRIVING

- Take a wider stance with your feet at shoulder width.
- Use a slightly closed stance. A line drawn from your left heel to your right heel should not point through to the target line but slightly to the left of the target line.
- Flare the left foot 20 to 30 degrees. Rotate the right foot forward 30 to 45 degrees.
- Position the ball off the instep of the right foot.
- Place the hands slightly behind the ball.
- Square the shoulders at address. Tilt the left shoulder so it is lower than the right shoulder.
- Tilt the body slightly to the left.
- Distribute weight so 60 percent is on the front foot and, 40 percent is on the back foot.
- Keep a relaxed grip pressure so the wrists remain flexible.
- Hit the ball on the upswing.

Setting up in this manner is easy to do. It will ensure that the ball position on the tee will be in the right location each time you hit from the tee. Incidentally, the height of the ball on the tee with respect to the driver face is also important. When the driver is resting softly behind the ball, half the diameter of the ball should be above the clubface.

FAIRWAY WOODS

Fairway woods are played much differently than the driver off the tee. The distribution and hand position being the primary differences.

Fig 6-3

Fig 6-4

- Use a square stance with more weight on the right side.
- Place the ball one to two inches inside your right heel as shown in Fig 6-3.
- Use a slightly descending blow (Fig 6-4) to make proper contact with the ball.
- Place hands slightly ahead of the ball. This will enable the hands to lead the club head into impact to produce the necessary downward swing path.
- Align the body a little to the left of the target line.

CHAPTER 7
THE LONG AND MID IRONS

LONG IRONS

If you are like most golfers, the long irons (1-4) are the most difficult clubs in your bag to hit consistently. They have the least loft and longest shaft of all the irons and this combination makes them less friendly to most players. The long iron swing should be similar to your wood swing. It should be a sweeping motion with a club striking the ball before the ground. If you can generate sufficient club head speed and make good solid contact with the ball you can be successful with these irons. Don't try too hard with these clubs. Approach the long irons with the same mental attitude as you would with a 6 or 7 iron. Use a slow take away and a smooth, easy swing. Don't try to overpower the ball but, instead, concentrate on rhythm rather than power. Don't reach for the ball. If you do, you can end up with a flat, rounded swing that will cause you all kinds of grief. Let the arms hang down naturally for these irons.

DISTANCES

The approximate yardages the average golfer can expect to see from the long and mid-irons (1-7) are as follows:

Iron*	Beginner	Average Golfer	Good Golfer
2	150	180	190
3	140	170	180
4	130	160	170
5	120	155	165
6	115	145	160
7	105	140	150

The fairway woods and hybrid clubs are quickly replacing the long and middle irons. They are very versatile and you can play them from a wide variety of lies. Because of the added loft and longer shaft, the ball gets into the air more easily and has less roll when landing on the green. Compared to the long irons, they are more predictable in distance and require less strength to execute a successful shot.

HOW FAR DO YOU HIT YOUR IRONS?

To see where you stand on distance you need to visit the driving range and practice hitting balls with each of these clubs. Take note of the average carry you are getting with each of the irons on what you consider to be good solid shots. Then observe how much roll you are getting after the ball lands. These distances are what you should use when playing your normal round of golf. When you are actually playing, don't forget to take into account wind conditions, the terrain (up hill, down hill), and the condition of the course, etc., (wet, dry) when you are making these judgments.

GENERAL SETUP

Your arms should hang straight down from your shoulders at address. The ball should be a few inches ahead of the centerline of your breastbone. Your feet should be at shoulder width, meaning the insides of your ankles are directly under your shoulder joints. Your body should be tilted slightly away from the target. The side bending will move your center of gravity behind the ball and enable a proper shifting of your weight to the back foot on the backswing. Shifting your weight to the back foot on the backswing will result in a natural shift to the right foot on the downswing. This causes the arc of your swing to move forward and will result in a slightly descending contact with the ball. To achieve the proper side bend, stand up straight and hang a club down from the center of your chest. Holding it firmly against your chest, tilt to the left until the club shaft points to your right instep. That's the side bend you should feel when you address the ball.

SPECIFIC SETUP ROUTINE

Place the ball 2-3 inches ahead of centerline

Fig 7-1

Tilt 6-9 degrees away from the target

Fig 7-2

- Stand behind the ball and draw an imaginary line between your ball and the target. Pick out an intermediate point along that line a few feet in front of your ball. This will help you to aim the clubface.
- Standing upright, place your feet together with the ball in the middle of your stance.
- Bend at the hips, and with the right hand place the club head behind the ball. Make sure the clubface is perpendicular to the target line. Complete your grip by placing the left hand on the grip. Make sure the "V's" formed by the thumb and forefinger of both hands point between your chin and left shoulder.
- Take a square stance and position the ball 2-3 inches ahead of centerline as shown in Fig 7-1.
- Check your shoulder, hip and foot alignment with the target line.
- Check your side bend as shown in Fig 7-2. Feel as if you are looking at the back half of the ball.
- Place your hands slightly ahead of the ball.
- Check your grip and relax the hands and forearms.
- Swing the club with good tempo and rhythm.

SIDE BEND

The side bend that you take with your stance will ensure that the proper weight shift is made to the back foot and as shown in Fig 7-3. If your spine is too centered, there is a tendency to reverse your weight shift to the front foot on the backswing, Fig 7-4, and to the back foot on your downswing. This will cause the bottom of your swing to move away from the ball and result in the club bottoming out too early.

right

wrong

Fig 7-3   Fig 7-4

IRONS OFF THE TEE

If you have a problem getting long irons airborne off the tee, teeing higher should give you the advantage and confidence you need to hit a good shot. Set the ball no more than a half inch above the ground. You want to make sure that contact is made on a slight upswing. If you tee the ball too high, you are likely to scoop the ball, and the result will be a shot that is hit high and a very short distance.

MID IRONS

The mid-irons, the 5, 6, and 7, are easier irons to use than the long irons. They have more loft, and the shafts are slightly more vertical. This makes these irons easier to swing. The swing motion for the mid-irons has more of a descending angle than the long irons, which gives the ball more back spin. The backspin reduces the roll of the ball when it lands. There is also less sidespin on the ball, which helps to reduce the tendency for the ball to slice or hook.

Learning to hit your mid-irons accurately is important if you are going to hit the greens in regulation. For most golfers, the biggest single problem with these irons is the tendency to slice the ball. Having the clubface open upon impact causes this. If the clubface is open, it doesn't make any difference what type of swing you have- inside out, outside in or straight down the line - the ball is going to slice.

SETUP

Make sure you use a proper setup when addressing the ball by using one of the pre-shot techniques described in Chapter 4. Look at Figures 7-5 and 7-6. This shows you the proper ball position for the mid-irons and the correct body position. Take note of the following:

Fig 7-5

Fig 7-6

- The ball is midway between your feet.
- Your hands are slightly ahead of the ball.
- Your feet are at shoulder width. The insides of your feet are directly below the shoulder socket joints.
- Your weight is evenly distributed between both feet.
- Your weight is on the balls of the feet.

Proper clubface alignment, ball position and a correct swing path are essential to a good mid-iron shot. Concentrate on developing a more upright swing action with these clubs than you use for your longer clubs. A steeper swing plane will allow you to hit down on the ball rather than sweep it. On the backswing, consciously swing your arms up toward the sky rather than around your body. Also, try using a slightly stronger grip by rotating your right hand over the club a half knuckle or so. This will help force your arms to rotate and square the club sooner.

To get power into your shots, cock your wrists early as shown in Fig 7-6. Complete your backswing in that position. Keep this position on the downswing and release your wrists at impact with the ball.

CHAPTER 8
THE SHORT GAME

The average golfer doesn't spend enough time practicing their short game. The general tendency is to spend much of their time on the driving range trying to get that few extra yards out of their woods and long irons. This is not to say that you shouldn't spend time improving your ability to use these clubs, but where you can get the most improvement in your golf game is by spending time perfecting your ability to make the short shots that you will encounter during a round of golf. Learning how to chip, pitch, get out of the bunkers and putt is essential if you hope to improve your play. In this Chapter, I will cover the short game fundamentals.

CHIPPING

The chip shot is what is commonly called a stroke rather that a full swing. It is commonly called a pitch-and-run shot. The clubs used for chip shots will vary depending upon the length of the chip and the subsequent roll of the ball toward the cup. When chipping, what you are looking for is minimum airtime on the ball and maximum roll. With all your chip shots, you will find that you will be more accurate the lower you are able to keep the ball.

Each chip shot is unique and requires that you use a variety of clubs to get the job done. Don't restrict yourself mainly to one club for chipping. If you do you will find that your chipping is often inconsistent and inaccurate. The club you should use for your chip shot will vary depending on what is commonly called the carry-to-roll ratio. Carry is the distance from your current lie to a position that is 3-4 feet onto the surface of the green. The roll is the remaining distance from the landing spot on the green to the hole. The pitch and roll ratios for the clubs you would normally use in your pitching game is as follows:

IRON	CARRYTO ROLL RATIO
Sand Wedge	1: 1
Pitching Wedge	1: 2
Nine Iron	1: 3
Eight Iron	1: 4
Seven Iron	1: 6

The following is an example of how to use the carry-to-roll ratio.

From where your ball lies, take a natural pace from there to a spot one pace onto the green. From that spot, using the same natural pace, determine the number of paces to the hole. Let's say your numbers are 4 paces from your ball, to one pace onto the green, and then 12 paces from there to the hole. The carry- to-roll ratio is then $12 \div 4 = 3$. This would direct you to a nine iron. These numbers apply to a fairly level green. If the green is not level, take this into account by using a higher or lower roll ratio to compensate for the upslope or down slope of the green.

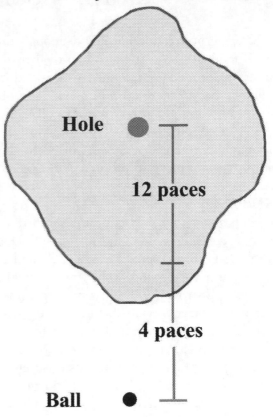

CHIPPING FUNDAMENTALS

| Fig 8-1 | Fig 8-2 | Fig 8-3 |

To execute a proper chip shot, follow the guidelines outlined below.

1. Fig 8-1

Move the ball back in your stance.

Position the ball off your left foot to ensure a slightly descending approach to impact with the ball. This assures that you make contact with the ball before the club impacts the turf.

2. Fig 8-2

Angle the shaft toward the target.

With the club head positioned off your left foot, angle the shaft toward the target so that the end of the grip is even with your right thigh. This will keep your hands ahead of the club head of so it descends into the impact. Keep the wrists firm throughout the chipping stroke. Some golfers prefer to use a putting grip for chipping. Grip pressure should be around 6 on a scale of 1-10.

3. Fig 8-3

Open your body to the target.

Use a narrow open stance. Make sure your shoulders, chest and hips are pointed right of the target line. Distribute your weight over your right leg This will assist in helping your shoulders control the motion of the stroke. Your weight should remain on the right leg through the entire chipping sequence. Choke down on the grip and keep the shaft upright, with the heel off the ground.

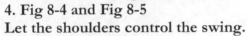

| Fig 8-4 | Fig 8-5 |

4. Fig 8-4 and Fig 8-5
Let the shoulders control the swing.
Start by tuning your shoulders away from the target. Keep your forearm and wrist firm so that the shoulders, arms, hand and club move away from the ball in unison. The length of your backward motion will be dependent upon how far you expect the ball to carry one pace onto the green. Your hand and wrist action should be minimal.

5. Fig 8-6
Keep the right arm against the right side
On the downswing, rotate your right shoulder back toward the target and then around to the right. For good clean contact, don't try to push the ball to the target with the club head. Instead, let the club head swing around to the right of the target along with your body. This will occur if you keep your upper right arm tight against your right side until you have completed your swing.

Fig 8-6

6. Fig 8-7
Breaking the Wrists

Poor chip shots can result from trying to lift the ball off the ground rather than hitting down on it. Make sure your hands lead the club head and that your shoulders, arms and hands move as one piece. Keep the wrists firm and the back of the right wrist flat. Don't attempt to move the ball by rotating your wrists through the impact area. You won't like the result!

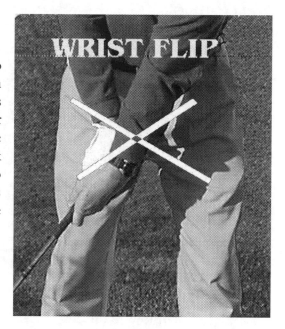

Fig 8-7

SOME FINAL THOUGHTS ON CHIPPING:

- Feel as if you are actually decreasing the loft of the clubface slightly through impact.
- Make rhythm and pace the primary thoughts as you swing through the ball, so the stroke resembles the even, back-and-forth of a pendulum clock.
- Keep your right elbow pointed at your right hip from address all the way through impact.
- If you are a high handicap player, avoid using a lob wedge. It will often hit the ground before it hits the ball, causing you to skull or chunk the shot. It also sends the ball too high to accurately control the distance. It is preferable to use a pitching wedge to become comfortable with lower-trajectory shots that roll to the hole.

PITCHING

One of the most important scoring shots in golf is the pitch shot. It is an extension of the chip shot but involves more wrist action. The difference between the two is that a chip shot will roll more than it carries in the air, whereas a pitch shot will carry much further in the air than it will roll. The majority of problems golfers have with pitching can be attributed to an incorrect set-up position. You don't use a square stance for either chip or pitch shots. If you set up with a square stance you will not be able to clear your right side properly. Your alignment should be slightly to the right of the target line and in open stance position. Your swing should be approximately a three-quarter swing rather than a full swing.

The pitch shot is one you would use from distances ranging from 70 to 100 yards.

FUNDAMENTALS OF THE PITCH SHOT

- Place the heels about 10 – 12 inches apart.
- Choke down on the grip.
- Slightly open your stance.
- Place your weight on your front foot.
- Tilt the shaft toward the target.
- Cock your wrist immediately on the backswing.
- Keep your weight on the right side during the backswing.
- Use a full follow through and finish with the front of your body facing the target.
- Control your distance by the length of your backswing and follow-through.

THE PITCH SHOT

●Move the arms and shoulders away from the ball in one motion.

●Cock the wrists immediately on the backswing.

●The backswing length depends on the distance you want the ball to travel.

●Keep weight on right side throughout swing.

●Short follow-through.

●Long follow-through.

LOB SHOT

The lob shot is very similar to the pitch shot. The major difference is in the flight path of the ball. Lob shots have a higher trajectory off the clubface and a steep descending angle to the landing position. These shots tend to be more difficult than the average pitch shot because it is harder to determine the trajectory of the ball. With the lob shot, distance is the most important factor since there is very little roll on the ball once it lands. To hit a lob shot well, you have to slide the clubface under the ball. This means that you must have a fairly good lie (ball sitting up in the grass). If the ball sits lower to the ground it makes the shot more difficult because there is a tendency to blade the ball rather than get the clubface underneath it.

- Grip the club lightly.
- Use slightly open stance.
- Weight on front foot.
- Position hands even with or slightly behind the ball.
- Position feet about 12 inches apart.
- Tilt the club slightly forward.

- Use a one-piece takeaway.
- Keep weight on the right side during the backswing.
- Take the club to the outside at a fairly steep angle.
- Cock the wrists as soon as you begin to take your backswing.

- Keep arm close to the body on the downswing.
- Control the distance by the length of the backswing and your follow-through.

66

The ideal club to use for the lob shot is a wedge with a loft of 60 degrees or more. As you address the ball, tilt your upper body slightly to the right, with your hands even with or just behind the ball. This will prevent you from digging into the grass. To ensure a shallow cut through impact, take the club back slightly to the outside and at a fairly steep angle. This will make it easier to bring it to the inside (shallow) on the downswing. Focus on the back of the ball. Take a few practice swings to get the feel for the shot before stepping up to the ball and making the shot.

PUTTING

The majority of all golf shots eventually wind up within 100 yards of the green. If your golf game is such that you are able to hit all the greens in regulation, then half of your golf game is on the green. One would think that if 50% of your score is on the green, you would spend at least half your time trying to improve your putting. But that is not the case for most golfers. Next time you go to your favorite course, notice how many people spend 30-40 minutes practicing on the driving range and how many people spend the same amount of time on the putting green. Normally what happens on your weekend golf game is that you arrive at the course early so that you can warm up on the driving range. Then a few minutes before your group is called to the tee, you spend 10 minutes or so putting a few balls on the practice green. Turn those numbers around. Spend 30-40 minutes practicing your putting and 10-15 minutes on the driving range.

There are only two things to take into consideration when putting – distance and direction. Of these two, the most important one is distance. **The speed of the putt is almost everything.** Even though your direction might be great, if you are consistently short or long on your putts, direction doesn't do you much good. *Therefore, it is imperative that you spend most of your preparation time on the green gauging the speed necessary to get your ball close to the hole.*

PUTTING STANCE AND GRIP

There are a variety of different putting grips that find favor with both amateurs and professionals alike. The two most popular grips used for putting are shown below. The first is a reverse overlap (Fig 8-8) and the second is cross-handed (Fig 8-9). Because these are the most popular doesn't necessarily mean they are the best way for you. I recommend that you spend time on the practice green and try the various grips to see which of them you find to be the most comfortable. Don't be afraid to change your putting grip if you are not getting the results you want.

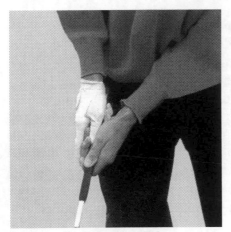

Reverse Grip
Fig 8-8

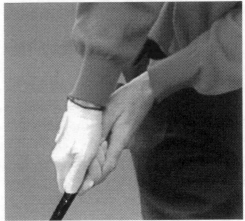

Cross-Handed Grip
Fig 8-9

General things to remember when putting:
- Always try to hit the ball the right distance.
- Keep the putter blade square to the target line.
- Keep your head directly over the ball.
- Don't move your head.
- Keep your elbows close to but not tight against the body.
- Palms of both hands go directly towards the target line when putt..
- On short putts choke down on the club shaft for better accuracy.

REVERSE GRIP

I will call the reverse putting grip shown in Fig 8-8 the "fundamental putting stroke" because it is the one you see being used most often by amateur and professional golfers. It gives you good control of the hands and the putter head.

CROSS-HANDED PUTTING

Many golfers like the cross-handed putting grip shown in Fig 8-9 because it tends to level the shoulders. This occurs because the ball is positioned off your right foot for the putt, and dropping your right hand below your left when you grip the putter forces your right shoulder down. This enhances your ability to swing the putter with a pendulum motion. Leveling your shoulders will also improve the chances that you return the face of the putter to a square position on impact with the ball. A cross-grip is an excellent choice for those short putts where a square putter face is the most critical element in determining whether or not the ball goes in the hole. The stroke for the cross-handed putt is the same as the standard putting grip. Notice that an overlapping grip is used for this putt. This grip helps to ensure the hands work in unison during the putting stroke.

PUTTING GRIP

For better control of your putting stroke, avoid gripping the putter in your right hand. Rather position the grip in the palm of the hand. Fig 8-10 shows the incorrect and correct hand positions. The shaft of the putter should be in line with your forearm so that it feels like an extension of your arm. This grip will give you better control of the putter during your take away and stroke through the ball.

INCORRECT   **CORRECT**
Fig 8-10

THE FUNDAMENTAL PUTTING STROKE

The proper putting sequence using the reverse putting grip is shown in Fig 8-11.

Fig 8-11

- Establish the putting line.
- Align the ball labeling in the target direction.
- Step up to the ball. Take one or two practice strokes to get the swing speed.
- Position the ball to the inside of the right foot.
- Put your weight slightly forward on the front foot.
- Position the hands just just ahead of the ball.
- Relax your arms and let them hang naturally.
- Keep your elbows close to, but slightly away from, the body.
- Use a light grip pressure.

- Keep the head steady and your eyes over the ball.
- Start back by moving your hands, arms and shoulders as if they were attached to sides of the triangle on your chest.
- Don't cock the wrists.
- Don't take the club back too far. There will be a tendency to decelerate the the putter on the forward stroke. The result will be a loss of the putter head needed to get the ball to to the hole.

- On the forward motion keep the putter head about ½ inch off the ground.
- Swing the putter head upward into the ball to to impart forward spin.
- Move the palm of the hand directly along the target line.
- Make solid contact with the ball by hitting it on the sweet spot of your putter (*p.58).
- Keep your head down until the ball is well on its way toward the hole.

70

*If you don't know where the sweet spot is on your putter, you can find it by doing the following. Tie a string around the putter and hang it up so it is free to move. Take a golf ball and tap on the putter, beginning at the toe and working inwards toward the center. As you start and move inward, the putter will twist. When you get to the sweet spot, it will not twist but move straight back. Mark this point. Repeat this from the heel of the putter and mark the straight back point. The two points should coincide.

CROSS-HANDED PUTTING
The proper putting sequence using the cross-handed putting grip is shown in Fig 8-12.

Fig 8-12

- Place the ball forward in your stance, just inside the right heel.
- Position your head over the ball.

- Move the triangles and swing the putter head up and into the ball.
- The stroke is made by moving the shoulders, arms and putter as one unit.

- Keep your head down after striking the ball. Look up only after the the ball is well on its way to the hole.

GETTING THE RIGHT DISTANCE

Spend most of your putting preparation time gauging the necessary speed to get the ball to the hole. One method you can use to get a feel for how hard to hit the ball on the longer putts is to face the cup from your lie on the green and think about how far you would have to lob the ball under-handed to get it close to the hole. Actually swing your arm a few times to get a feel for this. When you make the putt, use this same arm speed to stroke the ball. Try this on the practice green and see how it works for you.

DIRECTION

When lining up your putts, look at your intended direction from both sides of the cup. It is easier to get a picture of the break a putt will take if you look at it from all

angles. You also get a better feel for the slope of the green. Make sure you also walk the intended line to the cup to ensure there are no obstacles that can knock your ball off line. Mark your ball on the green and use the logo as an aid to establish your putting line. Align the logo so it points directly along the line that you want your ball to travel. Once aligned, pick out a spot 18 – 24 inches in front of the ball and along your putting line. Putt directly over that point.

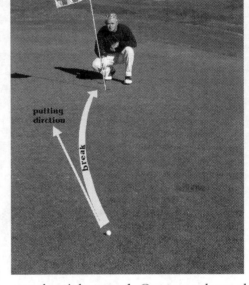

BREAKING PUTTS

On breaking putts, focus on one spot on the green where you think the putt will start to break. Then align your body along that line. Try to roll your ball over that spot at the right speed. Once you have the line and a proper feel for the distance, step up to the ball and assume your putting stance. Take a light grip on the putter. Take one last look at the spot you have selected and swing your putter head up through the ball, making sure the putter head travels in the direction of the spot that you picked in front of your ball.

CHAPTER 9
BUNKER PLAY

In any discussion with your fellow golfers about bunkers (sand traps as some will call them), most of them will tell you that this is one of the last places they want to be. Why? Because they have difficulty getting out of them on the first attempt and, even if they do get out on the first attempt, they find that they are a good distance from the hole or they have flown the ball over the green. Sound

Fig 9-1

familiar? Well, getting out of the bunkers is not that difficult. We tend to make it difficult and, therefore , build up a psychological barrier to executing a proper shot from the bunker. If you have watched professional golfers play from the bunkers, you will find they have very little problem with them. In fact, most of them would rather have their ball in there than in the long grass beside it. You should consider that playing from a bunker is just another shot you have to make. If you use the proper fundamentals that apply to bunker play, getting out of them will not be a traumatic experience for you but, instead, a routine shot.

This chapter will focus on the proper techniques for making good shots from both the green side and fairway bunkers.

Green Side Bunkers

The club to use for making successful shots from the greenside bunkers is the sand wedge. The design of the sand wedge is different than the other irons in your golf bag. If you look at the bottom of the wedge (Fig 9-1) you will notice that the leading edge is higher rather than the trailing edge. This is the only club in your bag that has this feature. The design has its purpose in that it causes the trailing edge of the club to enter the sand first. This allows it to move through the sand without digging into it.

EXECUTING A GREEN SIDE BUNKER SHOT

Fig 9-2

- Dig your feet into the sand (Fig 9-2) so that you have a solid footing.
- Assume a slightly open stance.
- Align your feet, hips and shoulders to the right of the target.
- Position the heels so they are as wide as the hips.
- Place 60% of your weight on your front foot.
- Position the ball forward in your stance.
- The club shaft should be slightly behind the ball.
- Open the clubface and then take your grip.
- Choke down on the grip.
- Use a light grip pressure.

74

Fig 9-3

- Bring the club back along the line of your feet. (Fig 9-3).
- Cock the wrists early to set the club on a slightly higher plane.
- Make a nice, even, lazy backswing along the line of your stance.
- Focus on a point a few inches behind the ball. Don't look at the ball.
- Bring the club head down into the sand 2 inches behind the ball.
- Concentrate on dropping the club lower than the ball.
- The amount of follow-through on your swing will depend upon the distance needed to get the ball to the hole.

To get the ball to fly further, adjust your backswing so that it takes a more rounded path versus one at a steep angle. More energy is transferred to the ball with this swing path. ***Remember, your primary objective is to swing the club head under the ball!***

BURIED IN THE BUNKER

A situation you may consider to be one of the more difficult shots you will face in a greenside bunker is a ball that is buried in the sand. Getting the ball out in this situation is not that difficult. It just takes a different technique than a normal lie wherein the entire ball is visible. With a ball that is buried in the sand your objective is the same and that is to not make contact with the ball. Move the sand and the sand will move the ball. For a buried lie, it requires that you dig deeper into the sand; therefore, you should use a pitching wedge for the shot, versus a sand wedge. You don't have to swing harder; you just have to make adjustments in your swing.

TECHNIQUE

- Grip the pitching wedge so the clubface is closed to the target by about 10 degrees. This will make sure the leading edge of the club contacts the sand before the sole and allow club head to dig down into the sand instead of bouncing off the sand surface.

Fig 9-4

- To adjust for a closed clubface, align your body to your intended target. Use a square stance, with the ball back toward the left foot. Pick the club almost straight up in the air (Fig 9-4) by cocking the wrists quickly; then chop straight down into the sand just behind the ball. You will displace a lot of sand (Fig 9-5) so make sure you have good forward momentum to clear the lip of the trap. The ball will have no backspin, so you will have plenty of roll when the ball hits the surface of the green.

Fig 9-5

PLAYING FROM WET SAND

Playing from wet sand requires that you change your clubface angle so that you don't dig down into the sand. With a square club (Fig 9-6) it is likely that the clubface will hit the sand and dig in too far. The result will be a dramatic deceleration of the clubface and very little movement of the ball.

Fig 9-6   **Fig 9-7**

Fig 9-8   **Fig 9-9**   **Fig 9- 10**

To prevent this, open the clubface (Fig 9-7) and hit the sand behind the ball on the back of the sole of the club, not the leading edge. On wet sand the tendency will be for the club to bounce off the sand and move upwards. To compensate for this and to penetrate the sand so the club slides under the ball rather than bouncing into it, bring your club up at a steep angle (Fig 9-8), cocking your wrists as you do so. Hit down onto the sand behind the ball (Fig 9-9 and Fig 9-10) with the sole of the club, forcing it into the sand. Use the same swing speed you would for a dry sand shot. You can expect the ball to come out of the bunker much faster and carry a longer distance. If executed properly, the ball will have ample backspin to slow its motion on the green.

FAIRWAY BUNKERS

There are five fundamentals you can apply to fairway bunker shots that will help you make successful shots from them. All of them are directed toward helping the clubface strike the ball before the sand.

1. Play the ball in the middle of your stance. Choose a club with sufficient loft to clear the lip of the bunker. Play the ball in the middle of your stance so that you make contact with the ball first, and not the sand.

2. Sink your feet slightly into the sand.
Maintaining stability in the sand traps requires that you establish a secure position so that your feet don't move around during your swing. Don't dig them into the sand as you would in a green side-bunker. Instead, sink them only enough to stabilize your stance. Then move your knees inward so that more of your weight is on the inside of each foot. Keep an upright stance.

3. Grip down on the club.

To maintain better control of the club during your swing, move your hands down on the grip about an inch. Choking down will give you more control of the club and will help you avoid digging into the sand before you hit the ball.

4. Minimize lower body motion.

There is not much room for error when hitting from a fairway bunker because you are trying to make maximum contact with the ball and very little contact with the sand. To make this happen, the lower body motion of the feet and legs should be at a minimum. Make a smooth three-quarter swing, concentrating on your tempo and rhythm.

5. Follow through

Your follow-through should be about the same as your backswing – about three quarters of a full swing. The reduced backswing and follow-through will lower your club head speed but you can make up for this by using one or two club-lengths more. It is more important that you maintain your body position and balance and not swing as hard as you can to reach your next objective, whether it is the green or further down the fairway.

CHAPTER 10
PLAYING FROM DIFFERENT LIES

It would be nice if every shot you had to make was from nice level ground and your ball was sitting up nicely on the fairway. This may happen frequently if you are playing on a nice level course, but most golf courses are not laid out in this manner. Frequently you will find your ball on a sloping lie rather than on that nice flat lie you would like to have. When this occurs, adjustments will have to be made to your stance and how you address the ball. There are four common sloping lie positions that you might find yourself in:
- an uphill lie
- a downhill lie
- a side hill lie with the ball above your feet
- a side hill lie with the ball below your feet.

UPHILL LIE

DOWNHILL LIE

To execute a proper shot from these lies requires that you change your setup so you can swing your club as normally as possible.

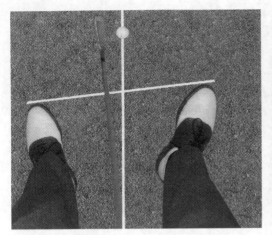 

Stance Position – Uphill Lie   **Stance Position – Downhill Lie**

Uphill Lie Technique

- Aim to the **left** of the target.
- Use a **closed** stance.
- Play ball about 3 inches off right heel.
- Weight slightly on the right side during the swing.
- Hands in front of the ball.
- Tilt your body to match the slope.
- Swing the club along the slope of the hill.
- Use **lower-lofted** club for a lower trajectory.

Downhill Lie Technique

- Aim to the **right** of the target.
- Use a **medium open** stance.
- Play ball about 4 inches off right heel.
- Weight slightly on right side during during the swing.
- Hands in front of the ball.
- Tilt your body to match the slope.
- Swing the club along the slope of the hill.
- Use **higher-lofted** club for higher. trajectory.

Side hill lie–ball below the feet   **Side hill lie–ball above the feet**

- Open stance. Stand closer to the ball.
- Bend more from your hips and knees.
- Weight on right side and back of heels
- Grip to the end of the club.
- Aim slightly to the right of the target
- Ball is about 4 inches off the right heel.
- **Use one higher club to reduce slice.**

- Closed stance. Stand further from ball.
- More upright stance.
- Weight on right side and on balls of the feet.
- Choke down slightly on the club.
- Aim slightly to the left of the target
- Ball is about 2 inches back from right heel.
- **Use one lower club to reduce slice.**

PLAYING FROM THE ROUGH

Playing from the rough is difficult because you are never totally sure how your ball is going to come out – if it comes out at all. The important thing is to just get the ball out so that you don't have to "try again."

It is recommended that you don't use a long iron for this shot. They are not designed for this situation. Rather, choose a club that gives you the best chance to make solid contact with the ball. The club will depend on how deeply your ball is embedded in the grass and the type of grass that you are in. The mid-irons and higher are the clubs of choice. You may not be able to reach the green with your choice of club but it is more important that you get out of the rough than it is to reach the green.

To make a successful exit from the rough, do the following:

- Position the ball midway between your feet.
- Use a square stance with 60% of your weight on the right side.
- If the rough is thick, move the ball back another inch or two in your stance.
- Stand a little closer to the ball (about 1 or 2 inches) than you would for a normal iron shot.
- Choke down slightly. Use a firm grip (6 on a scale of 1-10).
- Position your hands ahead of the ball.
- Open the clubface slightly. The grass will tend to close it as you hit into the ball.
- Use an upright "V" swing, not a "U" shaped swing. Hit down into the ball.

CHAPTER 11
ESTABLISHING A PRE-SHOT ROUTINE

The purpose of the pre-shot routine is to achieve consistency. It is an important step leading up to each and every shot you make. It is one of the keys to a lower golf score and establishing one will help you to:

●analyze the shot ahead of you so that you are prepared to get the ball to the desired location on the fairway or green.

●use the correct address position and posture each time you step up to the ball for a shot;

Most often, golfers tend to be focused solely on the mechanics of striking the ball, and frequently forget that not only are they trying to hit the ball solidly, but also hit it along a selected target line and to a specific location.

There is no specific pre-shot routine that applies to everyone. What is important is that you establish one for yourself and that you use it consistently throughout your golf game. There are some basic principles, however, that will help you establish a routine of your own. You can follow these principles and then adjust them to suit your game.

1. VISUALIZING YOUR SHOT

●Stand behind the ball and concentrate on your target line.

●Look at the ball and check your lie. Is it on the flat, uphill, downhill, side hill, in light rough or deep rough?

●Fix the target line in your mind and try to visualize the shot you want to make and how you plan to make that shot. In your mind, picture the ball leaving the clubface and the flight path it will take.

●Consider the target area. Is the landing area flat or sloped? Where is the pin located? Is the landing area hard or soft?

●Do you have a wind behind you, coming at you or coming from the side?

●Determine the distance needed to hit your target landing area, and select the golf club you need for that distance.

2. PREPARING FOR THE SHOT

- Take a couple of practice swings behind the ball, and then one along the target line to release any tension you may have in your arms, hands and shoulders.
- Address the ball by placing your clubface behind the ball with your right hand.
- Align the clubface so it is square to the target line.
- Pick a spot in front of your ball on the line that you want it to travel. This will help to make sure you have the proper clubface alignment.

- Step into the ball with your right foot. Place your left hand on the grip.

- Place your left foot in the correct position and check to be sure your shoulders, hips and feet are parallel to the target line and the clubface is still at 90 degrees to the target line.
- Take the proper stance (knee bend and upper body tilt).
- Take one last look down the target line to make sure you have selected the correct direction for your shot.

- Waggle the club a couple of times to release any tension in your hands, arms and shoulders. Once you are set up don't spend a long time over the ball thinking about what you going to do. Just hit the ball.

Make sure you don't change something once you are ready to take your swing. If you do make a change, your pre-shot routine should be cancelled and begun again.

CHAPTER 12
THE FLIGHT OF THE GOLF BALL

Two important things you must learn to control in your golf game are:
1. The direction the ball travels, and
2. How far the ball travels;

The direction the ball travels is of most concern to all golfers. If you can get the direction down, distance is just a matter of making the proper club selection and then using the proper rhythm and speed in your swing to get the ball to where you want it.

BALL FLIGHT
There are two things that influence the trajectory of the golf ball once it leaves the clubface - the position of the clubface upon impact with the ball and the swing path.

Club face - The three positions the clubface can be in when it strikes the ball are open, square and closed.

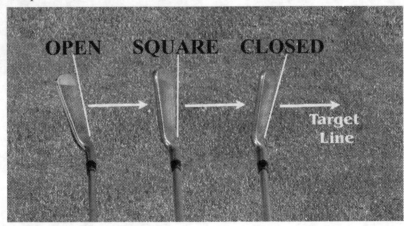

Swing Path - The three paths you can have are outside in, square and inside out.

Let's look at how each of these determines the path the golf ball will travel.

CLUB FACE

If the club face is perpendicular to your swing path there are three directions the ball will travel relative to the target line:

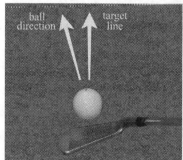 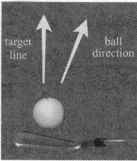 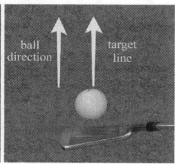

| 1. Inside to outside
Push shot | 2. Outside to inside
Pull shot | 3. Square
Straight Ahead |

SWING PATH - Perpendicular to the target line

If your swing path is **square** to the target line at impact, there is only one variable that has significant influence on the direction of the ball, and that is the position of the clubface.

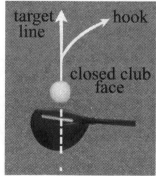 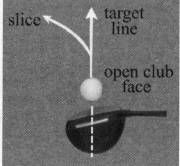 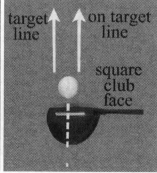

| 1. Square path,
closed clubface | 2. Square path,
open clubface | 3. Square path,
square clubface |

- In position 1 the ball will start out in a straight line towards the target. The ball will then hook to the right because of the clockwise rotation imparted by the closed clubface.
- In position 2 the ball will start out in a straight line toward the target. It will then slice to the left because of the counter-clockwise rotation caused by the open clubface.
- In position 3 the ball will travel in a straight line to the target.

SWING PATH – Outside to Inside

With an outside to inside swing, the following scenarios will occur.

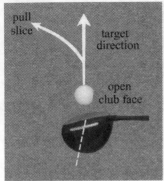 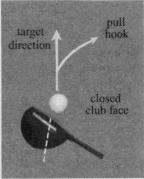

1.Outside/inside Open clubface	2 Outside/ inside Square clubface	3. Outside/inside Closed clubface

- In position 1 the ball will leave the clubface in a straight path to the right. Because of the counterclockwise spin imparted by the open clubface, the ball will then move to the left and result in a **pull slice.**
- In position 2 the ball will leave the clubface in a straight line to the right and continue on this line and result in a pull shot.
- In position 3 the ball will leave the clubface in a straight path to the right. The ball will continue moving right because of the clockwise spin rotation imparted by the closed clubface and result in a **pull hook.**

SWING PATH– Inside to Outside

With an inside to outside swing, the following scenarios will occur:

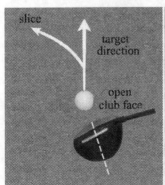 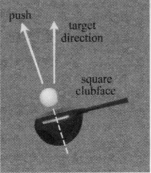 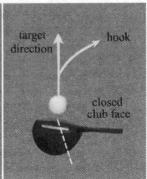

1. Inside/outside Open clubface	2. Inside/outside Square clubface	3. Inside/outside Closed club face

- In position 1 the ball will leave the clubface traveling in a straight line to the left. Because of the counterclockwise spin imparted by the open clubface, the ball will begin to slice and continue further to the left and result in a **push slice.**
- In position 2 the ball will leave the clubface traveling in a straight path to the left. Since there is little or no spin on the ball, it will continue in a straight line to the left. This is called a **push shot.**
- In position 3 the ball will leave the clubface traveling to the left. It will then turn to the right because of the clockwise spin on the ball. The result will be a **push hook.**

As you can see from the above, there are essentially nine directions your ball can travel, depending on two variables—swing path and club head position on impact with the ball. A summary of these is shown below:

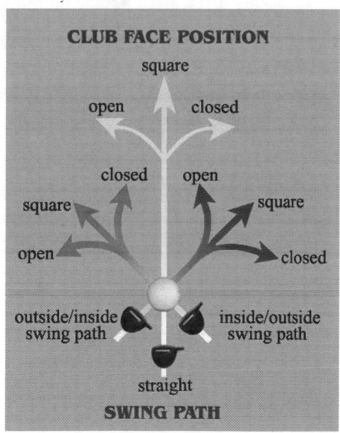

TRAJECTORY

The golf club you use and your swing path determine the trajectory of the ball and the distance it will travel. With your woods and low irons, the shallower "C- shaped" swing path will launch a ball at a shallow angle and the ball will travel further than it will if you use clubs with higher loft. As you move to the shorter irons, your swing path becomes steeper and the loft of the club gets steeper. The result will be that your ball will fly higher, but with a shorter distance than it would if you were to use your woods and low irons. The ball will also have greater backspin, which causes the ball to climb higher and travel shorter distances.

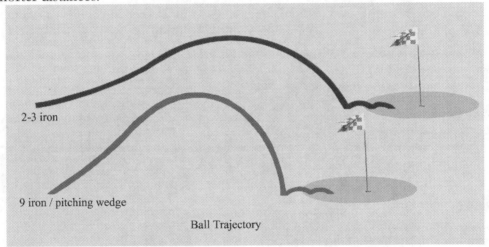

2-3 iron

9 iron / pitching wedge

Ball Trajectory

SHAPING YOUR SHOTS

One of the good tools available to you on the golf course is the ability to control the fade or draw on the ball. There are many cases where a straight shot is not what you want. You may have a dog leg that is conducive to a fade or a draw, a shot that requires that you go around an obstacle or a wind condition that favors either a draw or a fade.

To execute a draw, do the following:

● Set the club head behind the ball so the clubface is perpendicular to the target line. Align your feet, hips and shoulders slightly to the *left* of the target line. Be aware that there is over spin on the golf ball on a draw shot so the ball will roll further when it lands. Take this into consideration when selecting a landing area for the ball.

- Strengthen your **_right hand_** grip slightly by rotating it counter clockwise so you can see three   knuckles on your hand when you look down.
- Make a good turn on your backswing. When moving the club down, swing inside to outside so the club sweeps across the target line from left to right.

To execute a fade do the following:
- Set the club head behind the ball so the clubface is perpendicular to the target line. Align your feet, hips and shoulders slightly to the **_right_** of the target line.
- Choke down on the club 2-3 inches and weaken your grip slightly by rotating your **_right hand_** slightly clockwise.
- Make a little more upright swing. At the top of your backswing the shaft of the club should point right of your target line.
- On the downswing, the club head will have an outside to inside trajectory. The clubface will be open relative to the path of your swing thus creating sidespin on the ball.

One other method that you can use for a draw is to align your shoulders, hips and feet in the direction you want the ball to travel and then close the club face so it is pointing at the target. This will impart a clockwise revolution on the ball and force it to move to the right.

For a fade, do just the opposite. Align the shoulders, hips and feet in the direction you want the ball to travel and then open the club face so it points at the target. This will impart a counterclockwise spin on the ball and force it to move to the left.

CHAPTER 13
A LITTLE ABOUT BALLS AND CLUBS

GETTING THE CORRECT CLUBS

Playing better golf requires that you spend the time and energy practicing and playing. You also need the proper equipment to make this happen. Custom fitting your golf clubs so they meet your swing speed and physical body measurements will enhance your ability to lower your golf score. Professional golf shops have the equipment and the expertise to do this for you. They can give you recommendations for the proper type and length of shaft, the correct flex, the right grip size and the weight and offsets for your club heads. If you are a beginner and plan to play regularly, I recommend that you get yourself a good set of clubs so that as you improve you don't have to go out and buy a better set because the cheaper ones you bought just don't do the job.

CLUB SHAFT

Selecting the right golf clubs can be a daunting task, considering the numbers of makes and models that are on the market today. If you are buying new clubs and want consistency from club to club, then the shaft of the club you select is important. Just as the grip attaching your hands to the club is one of the keys to a successful golf shot, the shaft of the golf club is the single most important factor in a good golf club.

There are hundreds of shafts out there in both graphite and steel alloys. If your intention is to get your game to a higher level and you are planning to buy a good set of clubs, make sure you get shafts of high quality. Quality shafts are more expensive, but when you purchase them you can be assured that you will get shafts that meet exacting specifications. Good shafts will give you a balanced set of clubs and remove just one more variable from your game.

All major manufacturers have more than one shaft product line from which you can choose. Commercial grade shafts can vary in weight from one shaft to the next. The highest quality shafts are produced to exacting weight and dimensional tolerances, and the price for these shafts is always higher than the mass-produced commercial grades. On a high-grade shaft the major manufacturers will normally have a label imprinted on the shaft. Look for the labeling on the shafts that you buy.

GRAPHITE AND STEEL SHAFTS

Graphite shafts are slightly more expensive than steel shafts and they are lighter by as much as 90 grams (5 ounces). The lighter weight will help to increase your swing speed and the resulting distance that the ball travels. They absorb much more vibration than steel shafts and transmit less of the shock of a miss-hit up the shaft to the hands.

Steel shafts are less expensive and heavier. Many players, however, like the feel of the steel shaft and its responsiveness. The majority of advanced players use steel shafts.

SHAFT FLEX

Shaft flex is not a consistent unit of measure across all manufacturers. What might be a stiff flex from one manufacturer is a regular flex from another. The shaft flex to use is the one the manufacturer recommends based on your swing speed or how far you hit your irons and woods.

SHAFT LENGTH

Most golfers play with golf clubs that are of the incorrect length. Since there is no "standard length" for golf clubs, manufacturers can make them of various lengths. Buying clubs at a golf supply store or warehouse right off the rack, or on sale may save you money but it will not ensure that you get a golf shaft that is the correct length for your game. The incorrect shaft length can have an adverse effect on the lie of the club.

To determine if the shafts on the clubs you currently own are the correct length, do the following:

1. Set the club on a solid surface with the grooves parallel to the floor. Fig 13-1.
2. Place a tape measure behind the shaft with the end butted against the floor. Fig 13-2.
3. Measure up the shaft to a point that is 1/8 inch below the end of the grip. Fig 13-3.
4. Repeat this measurement and record the dimensions for all your irons and woods.
5. Take these dimensions to your local golf shop and ask them to determine if they are of the correct length.

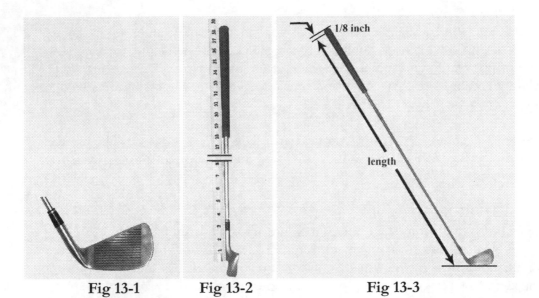

Fig 13-1   **Fig 13-2**   **Fig 13-3**

GRIPS AND GRIP SIZE

The size of the grip on the golf club is very important. If the grips are too small for the size of your hand there is a tendency to turn your hands over as you swing through the ball. This results in hooks and pulled balls. With grips that are too large, the opposite occurs. You are not able to rotate your hands through the ball properly, so you slice or push the ball.

The size of your hand and the length of your fingers determine the proper size grip. Take the measurement from the joint on your middle finger to the tip of your finger (A), and from the crease in your wrist to the end of your middle finger (B) as shown in Fig 13-4. With these measurements, use Table 13-1 to find the grip size that is applicable to your hand size.

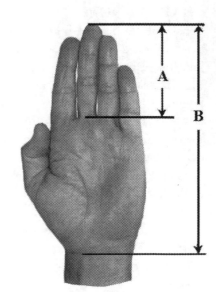

Fig 13-4

96

A dimension inches	Add	Subtract	B dimension Inches	Add	Subtract
2-3	0		5 ¾-6 ½		1/32
3-4	1/64		>6 ½ - 7		1/64
4+	1/32		>7-7 ¾	0	0
			>7 ¾-8 ¼	1/64	
			>8 ¼-8 ¾	1/32	
			>8 ¾-9 ¼	1/16	

*1/16 in = 0.062in   1/32 in = 0.031in   1/64 in = 0.016in
Table 13-1

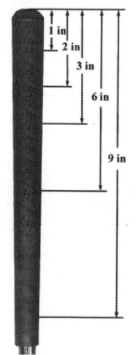

Once you have found the proper grip size for your hand, measure the size of the grips on your clubs. Do this by measuring from the top edge of the grip down. Take measurements at the locations shown in Fig 13-5. The readings for a normal size grip are:

1" down ~ 0.950
2" down ~ 0.900
3" down ~ 0.860
6" down ~ 0.780
9" down ~ 0.720

If the normal grip size is right for your hand, no change is needed. If it isn't, use Table 13-1 to determine the right grip size for your hand.

Example – If you find your grips are of normal size and the A dimension is 4+ and the B dimension is >8 ¼, add 0.016 to the normal dimension to determine the grip size.

Fig 13-5

CLUB LIE

The lie of the club (Fig 13-6) is the angle between the shaft and the sole of the club when the grooves are parallel to the ground. If the shaft on your club is too short, the tendency is to pull the heel upward while leaving the toe on the ground. This will cause the toe to strike the ground first and have a tendency to push the ball to the left. With shafts that are too long, the opposite occurs – the heel strikes the ground first and the ball will tend to go right.

CLUB LOFT

Loft is the angle between the face of the club and the centerline of the shaft, measured in degrees. If you look at the sole plate on your driver, you will see the loft angle of the club imprinted on the bottom. The loft on your clubs will go from a very shallow loft on your long irons to a high loft on your short irons and wedges. There is usually a 4-degree loft difference between irons, but there is no set standard for this.

The distance and height of the ball are affected by the loft. The lower-lofted irons will give you distance and roll, whereas the higher-lofted irons will give you height, less distance and more spin on the ball. Normally you can expect to see a 10-yard distance between irons, but this will be determined by the brand of iron you buy.

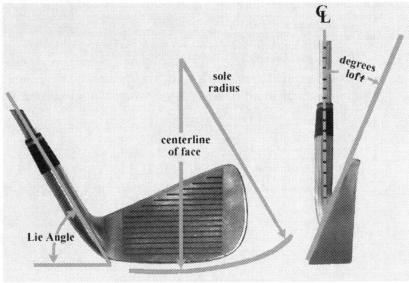

Fig 13-6

CHOOSING A GOLF BALL

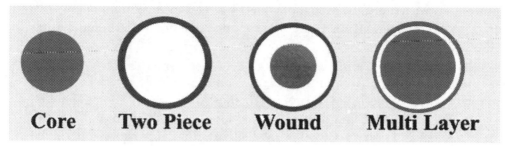

Does it make any difference what golf ball you use? The answer to that question is yes! Golf balls are designed to create distance and spin, and this varies with the golf ball you use. The correct ball can improve your game and lower your score. However, choosing the right ball is not an easy task, since there are a multitude of them that will suit your type of play.

At the present time there are thousands of golf balls that conform to the United States Golf Association rules. There are two-piece balls, three-piece balls and multi-layer balls. They have covers made of surlyn, urethane, elastomers, ionomers and balata. They have compressions ranging from 80 –100. They have different numbers of dimples. There are titanium center balls and liquid center balls. With so many choices, it is no wonder that the average golfer does not know what ball is best for them. So how do you find the one that is right for you? First, let's look at the construction of the golf ball.

GOLF BALL CONSTRUCTION

Two-piece balls are designed for distance and durability. They consist of a large core and a thin cover made from materials such as urethane, elastomer, and suryln. They have varying numbers of dimples, depending on the company that manufactures the ball. Because of its hard core, the ball will travel further because of the low deformation on impact with the clubface. It will also have a lower rotation rate, lower trajectory, less carry and more roll.

Wound balls are characterized by having an inner core that is either liquid filled or solid. The middle layer consists of rubber windings stretched up to 10 times their original length, and an outer cover. They are constructed for high spin and a softer feel. This construction produces a flatter, more stable trajectory and is made for the more advanced players. Wound balls are excellent for spin but lack the distance of their two piece and multilayered counterparts. Also, because the cover material is soft, the wound ball lacks durability. These balls are also temperature sensitive and the performance deteriorates at temperatures into the sixties.

Multi-layer balls have a large inner core, several thin middle layers and a soft outer cover. They are designed to provide the best fit for every shot. The core is designed for distance on the drives, the middle layers for full iron shots, and the cover for feel and spin. They offer good all-around performance in terms of distance, durability, spin and feel.

Cover geometry

All golf ball covers have dimples. Without them the ball would not travel very far. Depending on the manufacturer, a golf ball usually has 325 to 500 dimples on the cover.

The number, size and depth of the dimples influence the lift and flight of the ball. For shots where length of carry is important, use a golf ball with a low spin, as it will travel further than one with high spin. For approach shots, the greater the spin the easier it is to stop the ball in a precise location.

Compression ratings

The three most common compression ratings for golf balls are 80, 90 and 100, where 80 is the softest and 100 is the hardest. For those with a slow swing speed, an 80-compression ball would be appropriate. As your swing speed increases, the compression rating that you use should also increase. The majority of male and experienced female golfers use a 90-compression ball. The 100-compression rating is most suitable for advanced players with a fast swing speed.

Durability

The durability of a golf ball is determined primarily by the makeup of the cover. The three materials that you will most likely find for the cover are:

Elastomer – provides more spin and has good durability.

Suryln – this is the most widely found ball cover and has the best durability, distance and cut resistance.

Balata – has a softer cover that is excellent for spin. This cover is less durable and is subject to nicks and cuts.

WHAT IS BEING USED TODAY?

The Titleist is the most popular ball in golf today. More professional and amateur golfers use it than any other ball. Pinnacle, Top-Flite, Nike, Callaway and Maxfli account for the majority of other balls used. It should be noted that the high performance, multi-layer balls don't go any further off the tee than the two-piece balls. The advantage to the multi-layer ball is that you can get more spin on it than you can on a two-piece ball. The extra spin will help you execute some of your greenside shots where spin is an important ingredient of the shot being made.

WHAT'S BEST FOR YOU?

Beginner

If you are a beginner, select a low-spinning two-piece ball with a Surlyn cover. Go for compression rating in the 80-90 category. This ball is affordable and will have good durability and distance. If you tend to lose a lot of balls, you might want to buy used balls. If you do, select the ones you want and then use the concrete drop test. Drop two balls from the same height on a solid surface, and pick the one that has the best bounce. Some good balls in this category are the Pinnacle Gold, Maxfli Noodle and the TopFlite T flite.

Fairly Accomplished

If you are basically a bogey golfer but have a few spurts of par and an occasional birdie, you are probably playing in the mid-80's to mid-90's. The type of ball you need to use should be a little more precise off your clubface. If you hit the ball reasonably straight and are fairly consistent in your shot patterns, then a medium-spin 2-piece or 3-piece ball is a good one to use. Some balls in this category are the Titleist NXT, TopFlite Strata and the Maxfli Revolution.

Low Handicapper

When you have a good grasp of the game such that your handicap is around 12 or less, and you consistently score in the 70's and low 80's, you need a ball that is long off the tee but provides the soft feel you need around the greens and on the putting surface. If you are in this category then a 3-piece performance ball would be your best bet. Balls in this category are the Nike One, Titleist ProV1 and the Callaway HX Tour.

CHAPTER 14
RULES FOR PROPER PRACTICE

The tools in your golf bag have changed dramatically over the past few years and will continue to change in the years ahead. Technology has changed the distance golf balls travel. Club heads are perimeter weighted and made of high strength steel and titanium alloys. Graphite shafts are available to replace those made of steel. Club grips are available in numerous configurations and materials. Putters are designed to roll the ball more precisely etc., etc., etc. With all these technological innovations you would think that the average golf scores would have come down significantly, but that is not the case. The average 18-hole score for the weekend golfer remains around 100. For those more serious golfers who take the time to enter their scores into the United States Golf Association system (USGA) so they can establish a registered handicap, the average score also has changed very little. There is no question that the high-tech equipment on the market today can help to improve your golf game, but it will only help if you know how to use it properly. No matter what equipment you use, becoming a better golfer takes constant practice, and the practice must be done in a consistent manner. Those who have the time and energy to devote to practicing the various aspects of the game will do better than those who don't. Also, if you practice properly you will have the advantage over someone who doesn't.

Don't expect to see immediate and long-lasting results from taking a few lessons or practicing every so often on the driving range. Making the improvements needed to become better requires some basic changes in your mental approach to the game, and changes in the physical motions necessary to hit the golf ball properly. Long-lasting improvements in your game will come only if you:

- Decide that you want to become a better player.
- Are willing to make changes in all aspects of your game.
- Make time for practicing the fundamentals and applying them on the golf course.

The only practice many golfers get is on the driving range just prior to the scheduled game for the day. You can't make significant improvement in your game doing that. Your practice has to be done separately and always with a specific goal in mind. When going to the range, you should know what you want to work on and how you plan to do so. You should never practice without a specific objective in mind. Don't spend most of your time hitting your driver. If you really want to lower your scores, practice your short game. Chipping, pitching and putting account for about 65 to 70 percent of your game.

The following general guidelines will give you a routine which you can follow in your practice sessions.
- Start by doing some warm up-exercises.
- Spend your practice time on the fundamentals: grip, posture, alignment, balance and golf swing.
- When working on the fundamentals, concentrate on one specific thing at a time. Trying to improve multiple functions all at once can only degrade your practice session.
- When hitting the ball, make sure you are always aiming at a specific target. Without a designated target you don't know if your distance and direction are correct.
- Keep notes on the distance that you hit the ball with each club. You will find that as you improve and strike the ball more solidly it will travel further. The result will be that your club selection on the golf course will change.
- Establish a specific number of balls that you want to hit so that you don't tire yourself out. Overdoing it will affect your timing, tempo and rhythm.
- Begin your practice with a few minutes of "on the golf course" stretching exercises.
- To warm up, start your practice session with a nine iron or pitching wedge, using a slow tempo. Don't start with your driver.
- Once you have loosened up, begin practicing the specific aspect of your game that you planned for in advance.
- Use the pre-shot routine outlined in Chapter 13 for each shot.

PRACTICE AIDS
Plan to spend at least 60 to 90 minutes on the practice range. Break the session into segments with 30 minutes spent on either your chipping, pitching or bunker play; 30 minutes on your putting; and 15-30 minutes using a full swing with your irons or woods. Around the practice green use the balls from your pitch and chip shots for putting practice.

ALIGNMENT

To improve your alignment and swing path for your irons, place two golf clubs on the ground as shown in Fig 14-1. Point them along the target line you have selected. Keep the space between them around two feet. Place your ball in the center between the two clubs. Align your feet, hips and shoulders so they are parallel with the clubs.

When on grass, begin your shots at the front of the clubs and work your way toward the back. This will give you a more realistic lie because there will always be grass behind the ball. Keep your elbow close to your body when swinging your clubs. Try to brush your left-front pants pocket with your left elbow.

Fig 14-1

PUTTING DISTANCE

Getting the right distance on your putts is crucial to an improved putting game. If you are constantly short or long on your putts then you will always have the white knuckler on the next one. Practice your distance putting as shown in Fig 14-2. Lay out five or more balls in a line. Start about ten feet from the hole and try to get the ball within 18 inches of the cup every time. Once you have the feel for this distance, move the balls back 10 feet at a time until you are 30-plus feet away. You should be able to get a good feel for your putting stroke and the speed necessary to get the ball close to the hole. Practice this putting from a level, uphill, downhill and side hill lie on the putting surface.

Fig 14-2

PUTTER HEAD ALIGNMENT

Two methods that can help you with your putting line are shown below:

●Take your address with only your right hand as shown in Fig 14-3. Looking down the target line, align the putter face so it is perpendicular to the target line. Step into your putting stance, making sure your feet are parallel to your putting direction. Place your left hand on the putter, making sure that you don't alter the line you have established. This method of aligning the putter face to ensure that your setup is square is an excellent one to use at all times when you are putting.

●Place six tees on the green slightly wider than your putter head. Align the tees as shown in Fig 14-4 so they are on the line you want the ball to travel. Place a ball in the middle and putt it without disturbing any of the tees. This will help you improve your ability to keep the putter head on line.

Fig 14-3

Fig 14-4

SWING PATH

Your best drives normally occur with an inside to outside swing path (Fig 14-5) and a slightly closed clubface. This inside-outside swing path imparts a left-to-right draw on the ball, with over spin that will give you more roll on the fairways. The inside-to-outside swing path will also help to eliminate the right-to-left side spin (slice) that you get from an outside-to-inside swing path. See Chapter 12 for swing path and golf ball trajectories.

To improve your swing path direction do the following:

Fig 14-5

- Lay an iron on the ground parallel to your target line.
- Place a tee 12 inches from the grip of the iron.
- Place a second tee 18 inches from the head of the iron.
- Tee up your ball in the center of the iron, about 15 inches from the shaft.
- Set up to make your drive, with your feet, hips and shoulders parallel to the club on the ground.
- Swing your club so the head passes over the rear and front tees.

106

SAND TRAP PRACTICE

lines 4-5 inches apart

To execute a successful shot from a greenside bunker your club contact is with the sand, and not the ball. This requires that you hit a few inches behind the ball.

To practice your greenside bunker shot, draw two parallel lines in the sand, four to five inches apart. Place three or four balls in the center of the lines. Plant your feet solidly in the sand and practice hitting the balls by bringing your club into the sand at the start of the first line. Follow through so that your club comes out of the sand at the second line.

Film Yourself

One thing that can help you improve all aspects of your game is to see yourself in motion. With today's digital cameras, you can do this yourself if you have a camera that operates in video mode. Most digital cameras today have this feature.

Set your camera up on a tripod and, as you go through various aspects of your practice, capture it on video. Take the videos from the front and side so you get a good view of your set-up and swing. Review the videos to see if you are doing things properly. Save them so that you can compare the changes that you make as you move forward in your game. Again, if you want to become a better golfer you must be willing to put in the time to practice. There is no other way to make lasting improvements in your golf game.

CHAPTER 15
EXERCISES FOR BETTER GOLF

Golf is a physical game that requires keeping the right muscles and hamstrings in good working order. Flexibility of your body is a key factor in being able to execute a proper swing. If you are a weekend golfer or one who plays a couple of times a week, your muscles tend to adapt to the positions you find yourself in most of the time. For those sitting most of the time, you lose your capacity to rotate your body fully and your arms and shoulders are not flexible enough to make a full shoulder turn when swinging a golf club. Many of you have probably wound up with lower back pains, sore shoulders or aching muscles after a round of golf. If you don't keep the parts of the body that are used to play golf in reasonably good shape, you can expect to have these kinds of problems.

The exercises that follow are ones that will loosen up the muscles and tendons that you use playing golf. As you perform these exercises, you will find that your ability to swing the golf club and relax your body will improve significantly. The home exercises should be done three to five times a week. The best time to do them is in the morning, because most injuries occur when muscles that have been shut down for the night are over-extended.

HOME EXERCISES

CARDIOVASCULAR
Spend at least 30 minutes three times a week walking, jogging, running on a treadmill or using an exercise bike. This exercise will improve your endurance and strengthen your cardiovascular system.

ABDOMEN

Lie on your back with your knees up. Place your hands on your chest. Tighten your abdominal muscles and use them to slowly roll your shoulders up and forward. Your lower back should remain on the floor. Lower yourself back down to the floor. This exercise will strengthen your abs and lower back muscles, and help prevent the back problems that many golfers experience. Do three sets daily of as many as you can with the goal of working your way up to 25 for each set. Rest 30-60 seconds between each set.

BACK

Lie on your stomach and stretch your arms out in front of you. Raise your left hand and right leg off the floor. Hold this position for five seconds and then slowly lower your arms and legs to the floor. Switch sides and to the same. Do three sets of 10, resting in between each set. Perform this exercise three times a week.

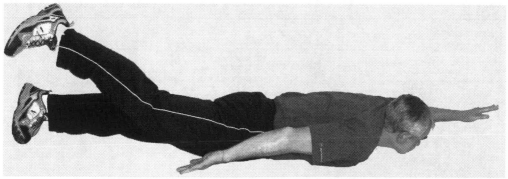

• Lie on your stomach with your hands in position to do a push up. Raise your shoulders until your arms are fully extended. Look directly ahead. Hold this

position for five seconds and then lower yourself to the floor. Repeat three times. Perform this exercise daily.

• Sit on the floor with both legs out in front of you. Cross your left leg over your right and place your foot against the outside of your right knee. Place your right elbow against your left knee and rotate your shoulders around as far as you can. Hold this position for 15-20 seconds and then reverse positions and stretch. the other direction. Repeat this exercise three times in both directions on a daily basis.

● Sit on the floor with your legs stretched out in front of you. Place your arms out to the side and bend forward as far as you can. Hold this position for 10-15

seconds. Return to an upright position and repeat the exercise. The goal is to get as far forward as you can. This will improve the flexibility of your hamstrings and hips. Repeat 3 times on a daily basis.

LEGS

To strengthen your legs and improve your balance, do the following exercises.
● Stand erect with your arms extended in front of you. Do ten knee bends going down to the position shown. Do three sets of 10, three times a week.

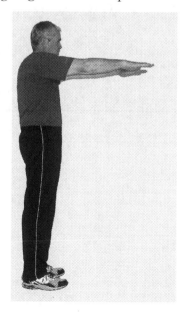 

● Stand erect with your arms at your side. Step forward with your right foot, bending as you do so until your right knee is over the toes of your right foot. Place your hands on your knee. Lift your arms in front of you. Hold this position for five seconds and then stand upright. Change to the other foot and repeat the exercise. This exercise will strengthen your legs and improve your balance. Do three sets of 10, three times a week.

LEG, STOMACH AND BACK STRETCH

These exercises will help to strengthen the leg, back and stomach muscles.

Lie on the floor and bend your left knee. Grab your leg midway between the knee and the ankle and draw it upward, at the same time raising your head off the floor. Pull your knee toward your chin and, at the same time, rotate your head forward as far as you can. Hold this position for 10 seconds. Repeat the exercise for the opposite leg.

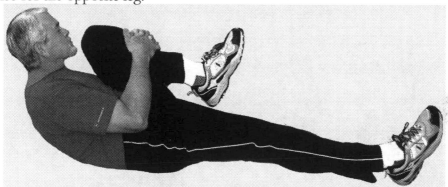

Then grab both knees and bring both legs upward and toward your chin. Rotate our head forward at the same time. This exercise should be done 3-5 times daily to strengthen and improve the flexibility in your back, leg and stomach muscles.

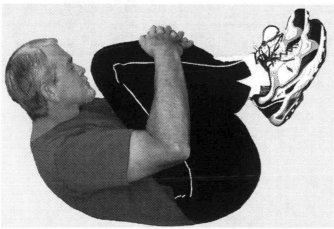

SHOULDERS

Weak shoulder muscles can result in an injury to the rotator cuff. This is one of the most common injuries in golf. The following exercise will strengthen the four muscle tendons that are a part of the rotator cuff.

With your arms at your sides, raise a 2-3 pound weight to shoulder level. Rotate your wrists outward as you raise the weights. Lower your hands to your sides. Do three sets of 10, three times a week.

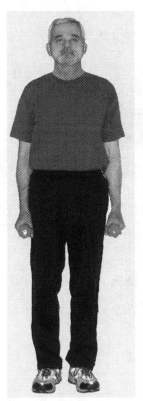 

SHOULDER FLEX

This exercise is directed toward the upper back and shoulder muscles. It will help to keep this area of your body more flexible and will improve your ability to make a full turn when swinging the golf club.

• Point your arm straight out in front and then rotate it 90 degrees so that it is against your chest. Grab your shoulder with your hand and pull it so that it is under your chin. Hold this position for 10 seconds and then do the same exercise with the opposite shoulder. Do three sets of five, three times a week.

About the author

Larry F. Nelson has been playing of golf as an amateur for over 30 years. He has attended professional golf schools and taken lessons from professionals at various golf courses in Arizona, Washington, Hawaii and Nevada. He is currently living in Reno Nevada with his wife and two cats and spends his time golfing, skiing, bicycling and hiking in the Sierra Nevada Mountains which are just minutes from his back door. He can be contacted by e-mail at "leftiesgolf@sbcglobal.net".

Printed in the United States
By Bookmasters